STORIES FROM THE CIRCLE

STORIES FROM THE CIRCLE:

Women's Leadership in Community

Foreword by
Fredrica Harris Thompsett

MOREHOUSE PUBLISHING
Harrisburg, PA

Morehouse Publishing

Editorial Office
871 Ethan Allen Highway
Suite 204
Ridgefield, CT 06877

Corporate Office
P.O. Box 1321
Harrisburg, PA 17105

Library of Congress Cataloging-in-Publication Data

Stories from the circle: women's leadership in community
    p.   cm.
  Includes bibliographical references.
  ISBN 0-8192-1536-8
  1. Women in the Anglican Communion. 2. Christian leadership—Episcopal Church. 3. Episcopal Church—Membership. 4. Anglican Communion—Membership.
BX5968.S76   1991
283' .73' 082—dc20   91-6754
                                                    CIP

Printed in the United States of America
by
BSC LITHO
Harrisburg, PA 17105

CONTENTS

FOREWORD

In general and particular aspects this is a path-breaking book. It focuses on an essential and empowering aspect of life in community: leadership. Happily and helpfully women are its primary subjects. Here the authors address a central liability in standard texts about "leadership" which too often ignore or trivialize women's particular constructions of leadership. Avoiding the dangers of "self-help" guides immersed in privatized reflections, this volume in fact reveals significant connections between leadership development and community-building. It honors at once the singularity of a human life and the central social dimension of life in community.

The book's primary context is women's lives, women's experiences as they learn new leadership skills through guided group programs. In these authors' accounts we see women engaged as whole, richly complex learners, persons with deep spiritual as well as psychological and other social aspirations. Moreover, the authors' general appreciation of differences among women makes this a text that will speak to women of widely different circumstances. Along with gender, critical components of race, ethnicity and class are named and addressed realistically and personally.

Most of us would admit that leadership is a critical component of human endeavors, yet how often do we stop to examine how leadership is called forth, nurtured and recognized as a source for new life? What is remarkable here is that we are given rare glimpses into leadership training in progress. Training events are described moving individuals toward new understandings both of themselves and of the wholeness they have to offer in community. The "bumps" along the way, the sudden "ahas" of new learning, the importance of recalling the past, and the desire for celebrating the new are portrayed in context.

For those of us who work in Christian communities, parishes and other institutions, this book offers experiential wisdom about leadership: barriers, opportunities, support and training needs. Readers of this volume, like the women who participated in five-day training programs, are enabled to understand group development and group process in the context of spirituality.

Stories from the Circle provides lived reflections on women's lives, women's leadership. It provides a resource alike for those women who want to be together in small support groups, as well as for those involved in building communities that are truly "comforting," in the best sense of this word, and "strengthening" for all involved.

Dr. Fredrica Harris Thompsett
Academic Dean and Professor of Church History
Episcopal Divinity School
Cambridge, Massachusetts

INTRODUCTION

Stories from the Circle is a collection of many stories about women who together are developing our God-given gifts so that we may become more fully ourselves. As we nurture our gifts of leadership in the context of a trusting community, we learn to value ourselves and others. We become free to define our relationship to God and to each other. From our brokenness, we become empowered—not only to serve God and the church—but to seek wholeness within a community that transforms ourselves and our world.

The Women's Leadership Training Program, organized and conducted by the Women in Mission and Ministry unit of the Episcopal Church Center, is one of the few spiritually based programs in the country.

The training sessions provide experiences that help women assess and improve their self-esteem, assertiveness, skills in management of conflict, the ability to be visionary, and their comfort with and use of power. All of this evaluation and learning occurs in the context of spirituality: focusing on the development of a whole person as a spiritual being whose identity is defined in relationship to God—not in relationship to males or other females. The larger hope is to bring about wholeness in the church, but this cannot be achieved with 68 percent of its members feeling they are not whole. As women come to claim all of who they are, the vision of the church as a whole, healthy, vibrant, and inclusive community has an even better chance of becoming reality.

The term "trainer," as it is used in this collection, can best be defined as a professional skilled in adult education, capable of communicating content and facilitating experiences that build the capacity for reflection, critical thinking and applied learning. In developing and conducting a women's spiritually based leadership training program, the women who make up the training teams have become part of an extraordinary process, one that has greatly enriched our lives and those who have taken the training. Our story is about us, our work, and how it has touched the lives of more than five hundred women throughout the United States.

Our first training session was held in January, 1984. Since that time, we have helped design a similar program for the Episcopal Church Women (ECW), the largest women's organization in our denomination. Called "Women of Vision," this ECW program has trained more than two thousand women and has upwards of two hundred volunteer trainers.

Our training has also been conducted in Kenya, and we are now designing a program for Hispanic women.

As the trainers met to work on this book, we described ourselves as "ordinary women involved in an extraordinary process." The extraordinary is experiencing God. It is about being fully alive and fully ourselves. Anne Wilson Schaef, a well-known lecturer, teacher, and author of many books, says that "God is process." We become part of the process by being in relationship with God, with ourselves, and with one another. One of the sayings that is told during the training to participants who feel unsure of themselves and the training is to "trust the process." In other words, let go and let God. To become a part of the extraordinary, we have to let go of all the "shoulds" and "could nots" and just be who we are. Paradoxically, this is at once the easiest and most difficult task to accomplish.

The five-day training program helps provide a loving and nonjudgmental community in which it is safe to let go of attitudes and behaviors that have kept us from being fully ourselves. It becomes a place where the truth allows us the freedom to gain new skills and knowledge about ourselves and others and to become spiritually renewed.

In developing community, it is most important to have an open and honest flow of communication with strict confidentiality. For in telling our stories to ourselves and to one another, we gain new insights as individuals and as a group. We call these insights gained from personal experience *learnings*. Through this process, past wounds can be healed, and new behaviors and attitudes can be learned that help us live into a new life and a new way of being with one another that is healthy, that is whole.

You are about to read personal reflections by the trainers on those sessions they conducted. We have added ruled margins for *your* personal reflections and notes. Please feel free to use this resource as a workbook, both individually and in groups.

We invite you to join with us in a woman's journey, and encourage you to share this book with others. In so doing, you will be developing your own community.

need to check again on feasibility of this training

THE PATH TOWARD COMMUNITY

Katherine Tyler Scott

I understand community as a capacity for relatedness within individuals—relatedness not only to people but to events in history, to nature, to the world of ideas, and yes, to things of the spirit.

—Parker Palmer
The Promise of Paradox

Those of us in the Women's Leadership Training Program have never been able to divorce leadership development from community-building—not that we ever consciously tried. Our belief in the interconnectedness of all of us permeated what we said and did. Each always seemed integral to the other, and the perceived partnership between them influenced how we defined the goals for the training, how we developed the training manual, and how we implemented our work in so many different groups. To the trainers, community is predicated upon vision, trust, respect and care for self and others, shared behavioral norms, and mutual support. Community, in the sense that we define it, enables people to reveal their inner selves and take the risks necessary to change and grow. We need to feel a sense of safety, and we need to believe that what we will achieve or accomplish in the end is worth the risks we are asked to take.

Most of the women who come to the leadership training want to improve in some way. They always arrive with a mixture of hope and fear, proportionately blended in various combinations. These are common feelings when embarking on a new journey or deciding to encounter the unknown. The staff and the participants must create a climate and culture that is safe, where fear is dissipated and hope is converted into positive action. Such a community nurtures the spirit; it does not cripple it. Even the most resistive or cantankerous person has a greater potential to become more loving and whole in this kind of community.

Learning to live, work, and accept others who are quite different from ourselves is so much easier to say than do. The leadership training provides the experience and context within which what we say and what we actually do can be compared and evaluated. The processes of community-building expose the incongruities between our beliefs and actions. The effort to achieve congruity, integrity, and wholeness is training in ethical leadership. In this way, community can provide the basis for helping us to become our better selves. Because community has the potential to be both formative and curative, we have intentionally designed the leadership training to maximize these forces.

We begin with a session in which we welcome each participant, share the history of developing the leadership training, and give each person an opportunity to introduce herself to the total community. The sharing of history is significant because it conveys the larger vision and purpose behind what we do, while informing the community of who we are. This is also a time when we as trainers model self-disclosure while conveying the guiding beliefs and values the training is based upon. As the exercises in this first session gradually become more risky, the participants are given another way to introduce themselves to strangers, this time through creating a name tag that conveys how they feel about their name. I have discovered what rich ground we uncover in reflection and sharing about the significance of our names. Creating "an outward and visible sign" of our names often becomes a grace-filled expression of our inner selves. In the sharing of our name tags, each of us gets to tell more of "our story." Our names are more than faces; they are who we are, and where we came from. We are immediately intrigued by the differences we see, and we are warmed by our commonalities.

Participants are then placed in support groups of eight to nine people, which they are members of for the remainder of the training. The support group offers individuals the opportunity to review and share their experiences and learnings. The support groups meet at the end of each day, and the sharing that occurs enhances connectedness and community. We then shift to another level and ask participants to share their hopes and fears about coming to the training. In every community I have worked with, this exercise has helped participants to see their fears as quite common. The very act of listing them on newsprint and saying them out loud simultaneously sanctions their existence and diminishes their power over us. It is, indeed, a cathartic experience.

The hopes of participants are then explored as we share the goals of the training. We look for matches between what we plan to offer and what is expected. This is an important negotiation between the trainers and the women in community. Participants are invited and expected to be full partners in their learning. For too many, this is a new experience.

The norms for our working with communities are simple yet profound:

1. Begin and end on time.
2. Use "I" messages—don't speak for others.
3. Be direct, open, and honest.
4. Maintain confidentiality. You can share what happened to you and what your learnings were, but you cannot share what others said and did outside of the group.
5. We all have expertise.
6. We are responsible for our own learning.
7. Have fun!

Participants are asked whether they wish to add other norms or to change these, and then they are asked to commit to those the community has agreed upon. After this, we review the schedule for the remainder of the training event and take care of housekeeping details. The evening ends with compline, led by the trainers. The community is asked to assume responsibility for worship during the remainder of the training event. This is done through a community worship committee that participants volunteer for. A trainer is assigned to this committee as a resource person. On the first evening, the training staff usually chooses to engage in a circle prayer that gives everyone a chance to express wholeness, energy, and connection. It is an appropriate formation to use in bringing the day to a close.

I have detailed the beginning session of the training because it is so critical to the development of community. The remaining content of the training will be shared in greater depth through the recounting of our stories in the chapters that follow. What is important to say is that the subsequent training sessions continue to reinforce what we began the first evening. We use the established norms as the standard by which we evaluate how we function as a group. They provide a basis for the trust and risk-taking necessary for learning. On the second day, we focus on leadership qualities, power and empowerment, the celebration of differences, and spirituality; we continue to work on a balance between individual development and community-building.

We ask the participants to work in many different configurations of small groups, and they are given consistent opportunities to process their experiences in the whole group. The continual movement from individual to small group community and back is a reminder of our interdependence as well as our responsibility for self-development and the development of the community. In every session, participants are given activities to discuss, analyze, and learn from. These learnings are then generalized to their home situations, so there is opportunity to look at how information can be used to improve the larger community.

So much of what we do takes place in groups that we feel it is essential for participants to understand group development and process. We share theory about the developmental stages of groups; participants practice observing group behavior; and they discuss ways to facilitate and improve healthy group functioning. For example, we talk about the phases that group members encounter when they enter a new group, the kinds of questions and concerns they are likely to have, and how the leader can be responsive to these concerns.

The primary question new members have about joining a new group is whether they are going to fit. Will I be able to stay, or will I need to leave? are the questions being weighed in the early group transactions. Participants are looking for signs and assurances that there is going to be a "fit." At this time in the development of the group, the leader must provide structure and be clear about the values and norms guiding the group. A tone is set by the way people are welcomed into a group and by the way they are given opportunities to say who they are. Once the decision to remain in the group (at least for the time being) is made, the next set of questions that emerge includes the following: How much influence am I going to have in this group? Am I at the top? Am I at the bottom? At this point, group members begin to jockey for positions of power in the group and may even challenge the leader. The leader who understands this phase and the reasons for such behavior can respond with sensitivity and appropriateness. In this way, the chances for destructive power struggles and win/lose interactions are greatly diminished. Once the group has successfully traversed this phase, it is ready for a different level of intimacy, which moves it into the third phase. In this phase, the question is, How close do I want to be? At this stage, the trust level is deeper and people are willing to share and risk more. The leader is less directive and more facilitative in encouraging the contributions of others. Although we describe phases, these descriptions of group life occur in cycles, for a change in the group's psychological life can shift it into another level and into a repetition of previous phases.

In one group, a woman who was initially feeling particularly dubious about whether she would fit parked her car close to the conference center (with her baggage still inside) and sat beside the double doors in case she would have to make a quick getaway. When she shared this with us, she had moved to the point of feeling comfortable and was much more trusting.

In every community I have worked with, we have a third day "rebellion." In groups of women, this takes the shape of behavior we have developed to a fine art because of our sense of powerlessness—passive and passive-aggressive behavior, a violation of the group's norms. A lot of this "acting out" occurs in the support groups, where we begin to hear complaints that should have been handled during the day's sessions. We encourage participants to be assertive and to bring up their unfinished business with the person or persons they need to. We take time out in the whole group to confront the situation and to engage the group in problem-solving. We invite candid comments and expressions of dissatisfaction about the training. We make every attempt to model nondefensive listening and constructive problem-solving. These sessions become "turning points" in the development of community. Inevitably, the community challenges and tests the norms; the trainers and the community both emerge unscathed. In fact, the relationships are strengthened, and there is increased confidence in the community's ability to solve problems, manage crises, and handle conflicts.

We developed a model that conveys leadership within the context of community. We refer to it as the "ripple effect" of leadership. It is a model with five concentric circles. The innermost circle represents the individual. The next circles are family, church, community, and world. Our work is to empower ourselves to empower others, to prepare ourselves to serve others, and to use the experiences and learnings from each sphere to develop and enrich others.

The trainers share their personal struggles to achieve balance between these circles, and so do the participants, who begin to realize that the pursuit of balance is lifelong. It is part of our very identity and vocation as Christians. It is a needful reminder that there are no simple or permanent answers. In the process of sharing our own personal struggles to balance self-building with community-building, these struggles become gifts to the community. Trainers become mirrors and mentors to the community: we reflect what we observe; say what we experience, feel, and think; and try to model health-inducing and growth-producing behavior. In this manner, we share with one another the power to change and to help shape the future.

Questions for Reflection:

1. What is your vision of community?
2. Does your "vision of community" include people who are different from you?
3. What are you doing to encourage the development of community where you live? work? play?
4. How do you balance the responsibilities for self-development and community-building?
5. How can you balance your own self-interests with concern for the common good?

_____

_____

_____

_____

_____

_____

_____

_____

_____

_____

_____

_____

CASTING THE CIRCLE

Ann Smith

In *The Meaning of Persons*, Paul Tournier, renowned Christian physician, counselor, and author, describes the importance between the personage (the sum of the roles we play in society) and the authentic person (a living spirit, both body and mind). It is his belief that the authentic person is discerned only in relation to other persons and to God and that both relationships are essential for emotional health and to experience the full meaning of human life. Dr. Tournier says that "information is intellectual, whereas communication is spiritual." I believe that, when I tell my truth through the telling of my story, understanding happens. When I speak from my heart instead of from my mind, I become a part of a spiritual process. In this state of communion with God and those who are listening with their hearts, illuminations of one another as authentic persons are revealed to us from God.

My feelings, perceptions, and experiences are separate from those of others: this is what makes each of us unique. One of the principles of the training and our work together is that we use "I" statements in all of our communications: *I* think; *I* feel. I remember when I was pregnant with my first child and the obstetrician kept saying "We are having a baby" and "How do *we* feel?" I knew that only *I* was having this baby, and I experienced many different feelings, several of which I chose not to tell him.

The reshaping of who I was occurred when I was married. I was barely an adult when I married: my husband was nineteen, and I had just turned twenty. During those early years of marriage and motherhood, I came across Betty Friedan's *The Feminine Mystique*. It became my salvation during a time when, not only did I lose my birth name, but I was beginning to lose "me," the authentic person. My roles as wife, student, and mother were overwhelming my need to continue to develop my own personhood. To complicate matters, any problems we had as a young couple—a couple who had brought an excess of emotional baggage from our childhood to our adulthood—were kept secret from the outside. We were both used to being the caretakers in our families and not letting secrets out. My father had died from alcoholism.

My mother had died ten years before him of a stress-related disease. We thought we could have a "do-it-yourself" marriage, one without the support and nurturing of an outside community.

My introduction to experiential learning happened at a workshop on expressing your feelings through the creative arts. A woman named Katie Newcomer, the Christian educator for St. Paul's Church in Cleveland, became my mentor. I had recently moved to Cleveland and was still in the grieving stage for an infant son who had died. Katie lovingly brought me into a community of women. And she introduced me to leadership training, an extraordinary process for healing and for growth.

That was the beginning of my new vocation to become a trainer. With Katie's help, the parish sponsored me in a three-year program for trainers with the Diocese of Cleveland. Through the training, I learned to get in touch with my feelings by beginning to let down my many masks. I learned to trust people outside my immediate family and to understand group dynamics. I began to get in touch with my authentic self.

My spiritual journey has been filled with highs and lows, with incredible moments of insight, with confusion and doubts, with laughter, and with pain. After I finished my training, I discovered that my interest was in working with other women. I worked for two women's organizations and founded my own organization before I came to the Episcopal Church Center as executive of Women in Mission and Ministry.

My first paid job as a trainer was for a community holistic health center for women. The policy of the center was to treat every client and one another with dignity and love. Here I first learned about shared leadership and the principles of empowerment in which all information and resources are shared and decisions are made by consensus. I learned that to tell the truth is to become free of deception, to be liberated in a whole new way of being with one another.

After several more moves with my husband and children, I went to work for Phoenix Institute in Salt Lake City, Utah. It is a community-based training and employment center by women for women who are economically deprived. Salt Lake City represents the most closed society to women because of the Mormon religion, which strictly confines women's roles. Yet in this oppressive system, I found the most creative and nurturing community. It is based on the circular power model in which client and staff equally share and are equally valued. Leadership skills are taught and all the "should nots" and "could nots" that hold women back are gently dispelled. Physical exercises, guided imagery, centering exercises, affirmation meditations, assertiveness, and skills needed for securing a job were all taught. Women are taught to release their feelings, especially the emotion of anger, in healthy ways.

I worked with a woman named Molly who gave workshops on assertiveness and anger. When she had crippling arthritis in her late twenties, a wise doctor told her that she must deal with her feelings of anger or be reduced to a life in a wheelchair by the time she was in her thirties. Having been raised a "good Mormon girl," she had been taught that anger was not an OK feeling. It took many years of therapy and a divorce before Molly became healthy. When I met her and worked with her, she was free from any symptoms of arthritis.

At the Phoenix Institute, I worked in a new training program that trained and placed women in the building trades. I cooperated with unions to place women in apprenticeships as plumbers, electricians, carpenters, and iron workers. In those two short years in Utah, I learned a great deal as I was teaching. This was due in no small part to Ginna Kelson, the institute's founder and director. She was also a mentor. In fact, the way that the Phoenix Institute operated was a mentoring system to me and to everyone who came in contact with this organization.

When I moved to Connecticut, I arrived with all that I had learned as an integral part of my being. I founded and directed a women's organization in Stamford, Connecticut, called Women's Work. Modeled after Phoenix Institute, it was designed to train and place economically disadvantaged women in nontraditional jobs. Although the organization was very successful, I made the mistake of becoming dependent on the state Department of Labor for all of my funding. As a pilot program, we could only receive modest funding for one salaried person, and funding was sporadic at that. I could not hire staff and develop a community of support. It was just too lonely, stressful, and frustrating not to be part of a team.

On a Tuesday morning, I declared my resignation to the board of directors. One hour later, the letter carrier delivered the diocesan newspaper where I saw the notice about my future life work at the Episcopal Church Center. The job description seemed to be written with my qualifications in mind. I believe there are no coincidences—just God working anonymously.

When I was hired to coordinate the work of the women in the

Episcopal Church, I knew I was prepared to bring to the women and to the church a new model of power that would help facilitate the working together of various women's groups. My experience as a trainer and facilitator of the circular model of shared leadership was what I was being called to use. Leadership training had been my lifeline in Cleveland. From my experiences with many different women's groups, I had witnessed how leadership training had changed the lives of women of all ages and backgrounds, from women on welfare to women in the Junior League. The church would add the spiritual component, which was not an intentional part of my previous training experiences.

I put together a team of women trainers: Pat Moore, who I had worked with in Cleveland; Dee Hahn Rollins, who I had met through the church; and Kathy Tyler Scott, who I knew only from reputation. We met for the first time in Salt Lake City. I wanted them to meet Ginna and then for the four of us to go up into the beautiful mountains of Park City, Utah, to create together. For five days we laughed, cried, argued, embraced, played, and worked together to develop a spiritual leadership training program for the women in the Episcopal Church.

As I helped develop the training, I remembered the wisdom of Ginna Kelson: the process is the most important component. A training program can have the very best of content, such as assertiveness skills, but if the process is not one of mutual respect and two-way learning, then the "synergy" does not happen. Besides content and appreciation for a process, we brought a spiritual element to the training: the deep understanding that process is spiritual when we are in relationship to God, to ourselves, and to one another.

The birth of the training program took place in the mountains of Utah. The first training session began six months later at an ocean resort in El Camino Real, California. The four original trainers—Kathy Tyler Scott, Pat Moore, Dee Hahn Rollins, and myself—sojourned together throughout the United States, presenting the training. Two of us took the training to Kenya. Six more trainers joined our program, and today we continue to shape an experience that enhances our spiritual, physical, and emotional growth as women.

As the lives of more women become liberated, so do the systems in which we work and have our being. We liberate our system by transforming ourselves. By creating a community of equals, we change ourselves and change our systems. We cast circles and not pyramids.

IN A DIFFERENT WAY

Katherine Tyler Scott

Timely silence then is precious, for it is nothing less than the mother of the wisest thoughts.

—Henri Nouwen, *The Way of the Heart*

The experience of developing and conducting a leadership training program for women in the Episcopal Church is a story important to share for several reasons. It is a story of many stories, each one flowing into the other like a network of rivers ultimately moving to form a body of water brimming with life and energy. It is a story of creation and birth, processes most women know something about. It is a story of power experienced in a form that inspires and enriches rather than thwarts or diminishes. And it is a story of spirit and challenge born out of a shared vision of what the church is called to be for all of us.

My phone rang on a cold, bright January morning in 1984. I found this familiar sound somewhat startling, for it interrupted the creative silence I was experiencing while sitting and sipping a cup of steamy herbal tea. It was one of those rare moments of quiet and peace in my life when I feel a wholeness and closeness to God that must be what sustains me during the hectic and demanding phases of my life. It was one of those grace-filled times when history is not a burden and the future has no fixed agenda. Contentment is in the here and now.

The caller's voice was unfamiliar but cheerful and intelligent. I listened with caution and interest. It was Ann Smith, coordinator of Women's Ministries (now Women in Mission and Ministry) for the church, asking me to work with her and two other consultants to develop a leadership training program for the women of the Episcopal Church. I responded with an unhesitating yes. Of the three consultants, I did not know Ann or Pat Moore, but I knew Dee Hahn Rollins, an old friend whom I had first met when she was a consultant/trainer at a women's counseling center in my community. Because I knew Dee to be a "soul mate," someone whose beliefs and philosophy about people were similar to mine, I assumed this would be a group in which I would fit.

Ann had described her desire to create a program emanating from the voices and stories of women all over the country who spoke of their love of the church and their desire to be of service *in different ways.* It was the phrase *in different ways* that caught my attention, for it captured the expectations and the emerging new image women were beginning to recognize and accept for themselves *within* the church and the world. Might this be the time to facilitate an experience in which women could learn to fully claim themselves and their unique talents and gifts? to affirm and prepare them for leadership positions that can make the church more serving and caring? The questions excited me! Having a part in the formation of the answers was intriguing. I felt the answers could be found and nurtured in this vision that I shared with Ann. The empowerment of others was my vocation (although this was not the word I used at the time to describe what still is my life's work). Saying yes to Ann was a recommitment of energy to this work. It was this energy I brought with me to Salt Lake City, Utah, where I was to spend one week in January 1984 working with three other consultants to develop a training program that would have far-reaching effects on hundreds of women's lives. Despite my penchant for planning, even I did not perceive the profound impact this would also have upon me.

I arrived at the airport in Salt Lake City on time, having used every ounce of assertiveness to ensure that I got on an overbooked flight. After meeting Dee at the baggage claim, two dissimilar and striking women approached us. Wearing full-length minks, they looked like my stereotype of Junior Leaguers. The blond was Ann; the brunette was Pat. I frankly wondered how well my newly acquainted colleagues could tackle issues of ordinary women, for in my first sweeping glance of them—in all their glorious gestalt—I saw privilege, wealth, and position. Remembering my mother's advice to never judge a book by its cover, I tucked my biases and first impressions away and opened myself to listening.

We all listened the week we worked together. I discovered in my conversations with Ann a shared vision and mission and the shared roles of wife, mother, and community volunteer. Pat and I were both organizational development consultants who felt committed to using our skills to serve the church as well as secular institutions. Often our different worlds fell upon us like the soft white clouds in the vast blue outdoor ceiling we looked up at every day. At other times they stood like the mighty mountains—bold, stark, powerful, and unmoving. Like the mountains, our differences had to be scaled in order to reach a point of coming together at our destination. Sometimes we heard with such clarity that our joy of discovery and new understanding encircled us and drew us closer. We talked until we reached a consensus on what we felt were the primary concerns and issues women were facing. We shared what we perceived were areas they most needed and wanted help with—assertiveness, self-esteem, anger, power, leadership, bias, prejudice, spirituality, sexuality, managing change, maintaining a balance, building community, and developing groups. Our discussions demonstrated that none of these were alien issues to any of us.

Each of us was also familiar with the many negative and often conflicting messages so many women have received about being female. While growing up, we heard that females are loving, warm, kind, supportive, caring, and sensitive. We also heard that females are incapable, overly emotional, unstable, weak, and "not-as-smart-as." Women who defied these stereotypes were condemned as "unfeminine." Accepting the stereotype meant a denial of self—a denial of all that we could be. To claim all of what we could be was to risk rejection and condemnation. What choices! Many women experienced "a different reality" than the one they heard, but there were few places and people they could go to have it affirmed. In the larger society, women found themselves through groups where they shared their stories and affirmed one another's journeys.

In the church, women grouped together for support in the service of others. Much of the pastoral and outreach work of the church has been done by women. We have cooked, served, polished, washed, prayed, stitched, and visited. Few of us came together for liberation of self, but at some point the problem of empowering others when we felt inadequate caught up with us, and the incongruence demanded resolution. More and more women were serving on vestries, standing committees, commissions, and being elected to diocesan conventions and General Conventions. Many women found their voices unheard. Still others found that they lost their voices when they were in meetings where men predominated.

The opening of doors and granting of opportunities was significant but insufficient to help women fully claim themselves and affirm their unique gifts of service. Having a voice means having vision and confidence, being centered and assertive. It means release from the tyranny

of fears: fear of anger, disapproval, loneliness, and the fear of rejection that plagues many women's lives.

Our challenge was to take each of these issues and develop them so that they were independent pieces of a broader whole. Because each is both autonomous *and* connected, their impact and usefulness would be even greater because of this interdependence.

On my return flight home I wrote a poem that came to me as I looked down on a feathery bed of white-on-blue with occasional prisms of light peeking through the clouds. I remembered our struggle to build community, the bringing together of varieties of gifts in a celebration of God that culminated in an offering to God and to the church. The poem given to me was "Prisms." I saw "isms" transformed by the addition of two letters just as we had been transformed by the addition of others different from us.

Isms
Fit best in prisms
Perceptions from different angles
Reflecting the light of truth
and brilliance of color
All different
and of Supreme value.

Changes,
bringing different hues
from scattered penetration

The light from within and without
So pure
So true
So lovely
So DIFFERENT

To block the light
Casts a shadow
To choose one lens
distorts our vision
While not destroying truth,
will keep us from experiencing
the wholeness of what we and
others are.

While not destroying differences
will create an illusion of sameness

While not destroying our spirits
will imprison them

Divorced from diversity
Robbed of richness
Exempt from life's fullest experience
Shallow souls in search

The power to see yourself and
the "selves" of others
awaits you
deep inside.

You have the power to
Shape the view
Create the angle
Reflect the light
Transform isms to prisms.

I felt we had launched a journey that would empower the voices of women and that, once these voices were heard, we would never be the same. The process of selecting areas of concentration for the training program raised some values and beliefs that not only shaped it but established norms for us and other consultants who would conduct the training.

We felt that many women continue to find it difficult to fully claim themselves—their uniqueness, their gifts, their particular vocations and offerings. We wanted to share our stories, resources, and skills in ways that would help women feel more confident, centered, and empowered. Armed with a sense of self-knowledge and power, women would be better prepared to hear the Word of God and interpret, express, and live it in congruent ways. It is my belief that followers of Christ are expected to be understanding of self and to use this understanding to hear clearly and to discern the truth—to think. In this way, we can truly be instruments of God and not puppets of ritual.

What we hope you will experience in reading this book is the same sense of self-discovery—in the context of community—that we developed in writing the training materials and in conducting training retreats.

When you disagree, argue it out; when you don't understand, seek silence. But keep struggling, learning, celebrating, and making a difference.

_____

_____

_____

_____

_____

_____

_____

_____

_____

_____

_____

WHEN A ROSE IS NOT A ROSE

Sally Bucklee

The moment we stepped inside Stella Niagra, the smell carried me back forty years to another Roman Catholic convent. But in the library I found *Daughters of Sarah,* an ecumenical feminist journal. And in the chapel's stained-glass window, I saw a woman included in the Last Supper. I relaxed. Clearly things had changed dramatically since I was the solitary Anglican in a Roman Catholic boarding school.

"Names" was the first training module I was to facilitate. Preparing for it, I gradually awoke to the role of names and the power of naming in my own life and identity. Beginning with my parents' naming and expectations of me, I was set on a course determined largely by my chromosomes and biology.

That night I was moved to look at how I felt about being called Sally Jane when my siblings were Madison Elliott, Craig Franklin, and Bruce Fairweather—names our mother deemed worthy of future presidents. Once when I asked about our names, she told me she wanted to bestow distinguished first names on her sons, who would bear a very common last name all their lives. In contrast, I would have Mitchell as my name only a short while.

Nonetheless, I always knew Mother viewed her third child, her only daughter, as a special gift from God. I wondered that night for the first time if there was any symbolism about the fact that I had come late in her life and that she had named me after her dearest friend, Sarah.

I was twenty-two years old when I finally received my full name. Was it a major transition like when Saul became Paul or Simon became Peter? Not in the eyes of society. Yet, like the unnamed women in the Bible, I was to take my identity from my relationship with a man (wonderful though he was) whom I had known only two years.

I felt anger welling up. I had been advised by the social security office to replace my middle name, Jane, with my so-called maiden name, Mitchell. In doing so, I had preserved the paternal name but sacrificed the one that connected me to my mother, Jane. In shrinking Mitchell to a middle initial, I also lost the source of a beloved nickname I had shared with my father and brothers since elementary school: "Mitch."

Nicknames are tricky. I have disliked every single person who ever attempted to be intimate by using "Sal." I thought of the gas station attendant at home who inevitably asks, "What can I do for you today, little lady?" And the men at work who call secretaries twice their age "girls." And how physicians call me "Sally" but would have cardiac arrest if I responded with similar intimacy—and I'm the vulnerable one, generally half-naked or more, on the examining table.

Naming has the power to diminish, belittle, reduce one to an infant, and control. It can indicate rank and distance. And it can also show independence, as when our daughter Elizabeth determined she would no longer be "Beth" but "Liz." At eleven, she claimed the power to name herself, and the name has stuck, despite my disliking "Liz" intensely.

At twenty-two, I thought Mrs. Brian B. Bucklee was a nice name. But it was not mine. Over the ensuing thirty-five years, I have grown accustomed to being Sally M. Bucklee. But Jane is gone, and there in Niagra, I named and grieved that loss.

Before going to bed I always turn my thoughts to my children and my husband when we are separated. This night, I remembered the fun we had naming our children before they were born. Jesus and John the Baptist were also named in advance—by God. God gave humankind the power to name the creatures. The power of naming is an important biblical concept: Yahweh's "I am who I am" and Jesus' "Who do you say that I am?"

By the time I was under the covers, I was thinking about the power of naming a fear or behavior and how, once it is named, you are able to exert some control over it. When I arose for my midnight sprint down the hall to the bathroom, I was thinking about how difficult it would be to trace the maternal side of my heritage. Thanks to our patronymic system of naming, all my foremothers are simply recorded in relation to men: as daughters or wives. Women, except the Queen of England, have never had a written history or genealogy of their own. Over half the population is without roots!

It was late, and I tried to turn off my mind. If I became this absorbed in every module, I would not sleep the entire week.

The next day at lunch, my rumination about women and roots became real when a group asked me to share my experience as a judge on the 1975 Appellate Court trial of the Reverend William Wendt in the Episcopal Diocese of Washington, D.C. In 1974, eleven women had undergone "irregular" ordinations—not sanctioned by General Convention—in Philadelphia. The Reverend Alison Cheek, one of the eleven, was invited by Wendt to celebrate the eucharist at his Washington parish.

At Bishop William Creighton's request, Wendt and his vestry postponed the celebration, hoping for positive leadership from the House of Bishops at its emergency session in August and then at its regular October meeting. Both times the bishops failed dismally to take a leadership role on the issue of women's ordination.

Throughout the church, women sought ways to openly support the priesthood of those women who had at last obeyed God's call, despite an ecclesiastical policy that made them seem more disobedient than obedient. Bill Wendt understood that, and what happened that November Sunday was not just about Alison Cheek. It was about all women. Despite ongoing support throughout the diocese for ordaining women, eighteen local priests determined Wendt was "getting away with murder" and should be dealt with in the ecclesiastical courts.

My listeners, spellbound around the table, were incensed to learn that the lower court split along clergy-lay lines, with all the clergy voting guilty and all the laity, not guilty. Clergy outnumbered laity. The Appellate Court divided four to three along male-female lines—and men outnumbered women.

The church never deigned to try any of the women, but it did so unofficially, and they were marked with a scarlet "o" for years to come. Bill Wendt was censured by his diocesan bishop in January 1976, nine months prior to the General Convention approving the ordination of women to the priesthood and episcopacy. He was the first and only man in our church to receive such a judgment, they say. His plea had been that he obeyed his conscience.

Later the House of Bishops, meeting in Port St. Luce, Florida, declared that bishops were justified in deciding whether to ordain women on the basis of conscience. In other words, it was permissible in this church to discriminate solely on the basis of gender. Oh, how the men of God hate women!

The tribulations of the 1970s were new to these women, some of them my age, who were listening to me tell this story. They were as hungry for stories of yesteryear's agonies as for knowledge of women in the Bible and church history. Learning the "her story" changes women's views of the institutional church and of their foremothers who actively struggled in both church and society. It changes how they view the present and future, when—God willing—women will be fully functioning throughout the church wherever their gifts fit. And people will know it is as wrong to discriminate by sex as it is by race.

As Dorothy Brittain told the group later, "The important thing about leadership is to do the will of God here on earth—and sometimes your own as well."

Over the next two days, I watched the newly arrived participants jockey for power as the conference design began to build the capacity for a spiritual community to develop. We were still in the "pseudocommunity" state of avoiding conflict, but some cliques were forming and acting out a counterdependence. We were a diverse group of individuals, each working out her own personal life experience with God. Would this training session—called Leadership '87—give us that rare opportunity to transcend our individual differences and come together in love as the Body of Christ? Would we four trainers touch these women at some meaningful level to heighten their sense of God's call and enable them to respond? Would it be worth using up five days of my very precious vacation time? It would, if the miracle of community happened—the kind that had pulled followers like a magnet to the early church.

A goal of each conference is to build community. Toward that goal, women meet regularly in small groups that function as support systems or minilaboratories for trying out new ideas and behaviors with feedback from the group. From the outset, there were problems in my small group. One woman was blatantly displaying behaviors that mitigated against the development of a support group. Another woman, somewhat older, was passive, participating very little. She confided to me that she had expected lectures. Still another participant, Anna, was clearly not comfortable being at the conference.

The first morning, Anna was frantic to leave despite urgings from several friends to give it a little more time. (I have changed the names of participants to protect their privacy.) She would not speak directly to any of the trainers, but we learned from women in her parish that her husband was to pick her up late in the day. She planned to stay in her room and simply slip out unannounced. Her reason for leaving was that we were "too religious."

As one who shrinks from confrontation, I could understand Anna's desire to flee unnoticed. Yet I also knew the support group and I needed

some closure—and I suspected Anna probably did, too. The trainers caucused. Our focus was on what seemed best for Anna and the community as a whole. This could be a valuable—even a transforming—moment for Anna to come to terms with her own self and be accountable to the community for her action. We could model how to "speak the truth in love." Dorothy and Linda Grenz, our third trainer, took the lead, helping Anna clarify and "own" her decision to leave. They assured her that she would be comfortable back home in the parish when her friends returned. I've since wondered whether that intervention has made a difference in Anna's life. Regardless, the risk, vulnerability, accountability, healing, and grace in that brief encounter provided a vivid model of living as if love matters most. The genesis of community was present.

One morning when breakfast was not ready at the usual hour, Dorothy called our attention to the sister assigned to serve our meals. Since our arrival, these chores were definitely not to her liking. Gradually we learned she was a master's level nurse, eager for a reassignment to a major holistic health care center. We resolved to make her job as easy as we could. Dorothy reminded us how many women have risen up on the backs of other women, to whom we pay a low wage to clean our homes, prepare our food, and care for our children. Our room and board in this convent was inexpensive because religious women kept it that way, but at what cost to themselves.

My early morning training module was called "A Spiritual Tool Shop." I opened with a metaphor:

> I am a tattered, 150-year-old house. Some years ago I was abandoned when a superhighway came through. I am a house with feelings, and I have been lonely and cold and empty. Many of my windows to the world have been shattered by stones and BB guns.
>
> Recently someone bought me and began to rewire me. I have new plumbing, paint, shutters. I feel acutely all of this going on inside me. It is very painful. But I try to bear it, because I know when it is done a family will live in me and love me and bring happiness and joy to me once again.

Renovation is going on in our lives here at Stella Niagra. God is ripping up our insides, or at least mine. Dialogue with God—prayer—is the beginning of our transformation. From the comments received, the old house was an accurate reflection of how life was for many at the midway point of the training session.

I could hear and see changes in women, even in body language. A trio from one church was absorbed throughout dinner with how to integrate their jobs, families, church, and PTA under the umbrella of faith: no more schizophrenia splitting the material world from the spiritual world. Women were talking comfortably across generations. Stereotypes were tumbling. The nurture of a non-judgmental, caring environment was stimulating blossoms everywhere. An older woman in my support group, with caring confrontation, shared how a younger person's behavior was adversely affecting others. Confidences were shared on walks or over a glass of wine before bed. There was a softening—an awareness of "the Absent One who is powerfully present," in the words of the theologian Walter Brueggemann.

A woman in her twenties bared her fears about her husband's obsessively controlling behavior and his insistence that she never be away from their young child. Her being there, sharing her burden, seemed a sign of the Spirit's intervention. And we who were with her that afternoon were God's agents, helping her name and claim her own needs and feelings.

Through it all, I had the sense of God as the nursing mother, feeding hungry Christians who must be weaned to meat and potatoes by the last day. We prepared them for reentry into their families, work, neighborhoods, and churches. And the last night, they roasted us. The walls were coated with bumper-sticker slogans they had created:

- '87 Leaders Do It Assertively
- Episcopal Women Do It in Circles
- Just when you thought it was safe to follow . . .
- Leadership '87: Stairway to Heaven
- It's OK to be where you are, but you don't have to stay there.

Nearly a year after Stella Niagra, I received a letter from a woman I had met there. She brought me up to date on how she was using her skills in myriad ways and then wrote the following:

. . . what I am getting at is that terrific release that I felt at Leadership '87 and the change ever since in my feeling about myself. You really do get warped living with alcoholism, and for most of those years you don't know what is happening to you. You think, and he tells you, that you are a terrible person. I worked sixteen years as a partner in a firm of consulting engineers after graduating from college. I am not a dope, and yet I kept saying to myself, "I've lost Martha," and I didn't know what to do about it, feeling that I wasn't worth anything anymore.

Enter Al-Anon, and my own recognition that John was the one with the problem and that I was responsible for my own recovery. And I really worked at it. And I think, but I'm not even sure yet, that what happened to me at Leadership '87 was the realization that I had found Martha. The MBTI information did it. For years in working with the Al-Anon program and living with either active or recovering alcoholism, I was trying to change myself. And then, in innocently answering those questions propped up in bed that first evening, and then answering the questions with the whole group the next day, I suddenly found I was the person I thought I was—I had found Martha. I can't tell you the release I felt.

I went to Leadership '87 to fulfill my obligation to my diocese and get away from the household routines, and I was liberated—just when I thought I was where I wanted to be. . . .

I'll let you go, but you know I will always be grateful to you, and now you know an inkling of why!

Questions for Reflection
1. How did you get your name?
2. What thoughts and feelings do you have about your name?
3. Would you like to change your name? If yes, what name would you choose? If not, why?
4. Would you like others to have your name?
5. What has happened to you as a result of having your name?
6. When have you experienced being belittled or diminished by someone's use of your first name or "honey" or a similar word?
7. What did you do? When have you experienced "naming" or owning something that was bothering you? How did that feel?
8. Share a time when you have felt the sense of a true community.
9. What were some of the elements of that community?

PARDON ME, YOUR *J* IS SHOWING

Katherine Tyler Scott

We focus a great deal on empowerment in the leadership training program. Much of what we do has the intent of enabling the women we work with to affirm and celebrate themselves and others in all of their uniqueness and diversity. One of the most fun and nonthreatening ways to begin to do this is through the use of the Myers-Briggs Type Indicator (MBTI).

The Myers-Briggs Type Indicator is a self-reporting instrument that measures personality type. The result of over forty years of research, it was developed by a mother and daughter who were deeply interested in discovering and understanding why and how people differed. Both women were committed to the use of the MBTI as a tool that would enable people to develop respect for their differences and to use their understanding to work more effectively with others. Their stories and their efforts to develop this instrument are powerful models of leadership for the women who attend the training.

Based upon Jungian theory, the MBTI is predicated upon the belief that human behavior is not due to chance but is, in fact, the logical result of basic, observable, measurable differences. These differences in our behavior result from innate preferences in (1) how we perceive things, people, occurrences, and ideas; and (2) how we come to conclusions about our perceptions. The MBTI measures these preferences in perception and judgment. Our preferences are not good or bad, right or wrong; they are expressions of our uniqueness as human beings. The intent of the MBTI is to help us value and respect these individual differences.

There are four preference scales in the MBTI. By completing a written exercise involving multiple-choice questions, participants arrive at their own preferences on each of these four scales. Their preferences are designated by four letters. The four letters combined are that person's personality type.

Example:

Scale I.	Extroversion ——————— Introversion
Scale II.	Sensing ——————— Intuition
Scale III.	Thinking ——————— Feeling
Scale IV.	Perceiving ——————— Judging

The extroversion/introversion scale measures energy flow. Those who prefer extroversion obtain energy from the *outer* world of people, events, and things. Those who prefer introversion receive their energy from the *inner* world of ideas and thoughts. I prefer extroversion, and interaction with people reenergizes me. I can be physically exhausted but can soon be at peak energy if I am put in a room of interesting people. Dorothy Brittain prefers introversion, and being in this same room of people can drain her energy. She knows she must plan quiet reflective time for herself during our highly interactive leadership training.

Our own differences have helped us plan training sessions. A good example is that the designers of the leadership training program were high *E*'s! As a result, it took several training sessions and feedback from participants for us to really hear how those who preferred introversion needed more space and time to integrate the exercises we had planned. We had discussed having time for reflection and meditation, but we learned that someone who prefers extroversion may not have the same definition of reflection and meditation as a person who prefers introversion. With this in mind, we try to be respectful and sensitive to such differences.

We found that even our definitions of spirituality depended on our personality types. For someone who has a strong preference for extroversion, spirituality usually involves conversation, recitation of Scripture, or some external activity. For example, Ann can feel spiritual while running across a tennis court and sending a ball sailing across the net. Someone who prefers introversion might experience spirituality through quiet days, reading, and silent prayer. Without an understanding of type and preferences we can easily become judgmental about spirituality. There are no fixed prescriptions for how we experience God but an infinite variety of ways greatly influenced by our unique personality preferences. The session on the MBTI introduces participants to a full knowledge of self and plants the seed for continued appreciation of "differentness."

The sensing intuition scale measures preference for gathering data. If you are a sensing type, you prefer to gather information through your five senses: sight, smell, touch, taste, and hearing. Facts are reality to sensing types. Although sensing types are grounded in the here and now, their memory for facts makes them good sources of past information. I usually describe them as "the historians"; they can describe the fundraiser five years ago, how many people attended, and how much money was made. People who prefer intuition gather their information through a "sixth sense." They are visionary types who see relationships between and beyond the facts—the "big picture." Their way of "knowing" is just as valid as that of the sensing type, but they'll have a more difficult time in a society that wants *proof* that their idea will work. Intuitives enjoy global thinking, as well as spontaneous and creative theorizing. My preference is intuitive. Unless sensing and intuitive types understand and respect their differences, the different ways they take in information can end up creating impasses and power struggles in groups. One participant experienced an incredible "Aha!" moment (a powerful revelation) when she realized that her conflict with her Episcopal Church Women board was in many ways due to her intuitive and sweeping view of issues. For the first time, she stopped personalizing the conflict and opened herself up to other possible explanations and solutions.

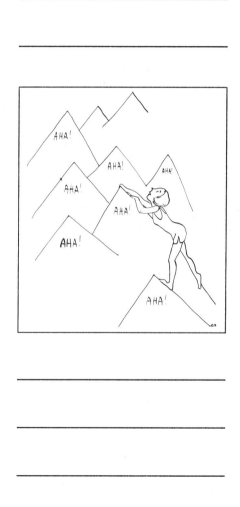

The third scale, thinking/feeling, measures preference for making decisions. Those who prefer thinking make decisions based upon what is fair, just, and for the greater good of the whole. They are guided by eternal verities in the form of rules and like to operate with congruity and consistency. Thinking-preferenced people are usually able to reprimand, fire, and manage conflict without serious stress. Those who prefer feeling make their decisions based upon *how* people will feel about or be affected by the decision. They are concerned with group harmony, abhor conflict, and seek to keep the peace. Their eternal verities are expressed in the form of deeply held values that guide them in their decision making.

As a *T* (thinking type), I make decisions that "make sense" according to sound criteria. People who prefer feeling believe they are also making decisions based on sound criteria; i.e., how they feel about it. *T*'s can be seen as cold and unfeeling, while *F*'s (feeling types) can be viewed as soft-hearted and wishy-washy. Once we realize how differently we make decisions, we can better understand each other and why our attempts at communication have failed so miserably at times. Thinking types have feelings, and feeling types can think, and we learn to consider content (the what) and process (the how) when we make decisions. We need both clarity about *problems* and an understanding of *people*.

The last scale is the judging/perceiving scale, which measures preference for attaining closure. If you prefer judging, you have a high need for closure. Judging types like things to be decided, planned, and orderly. They're the ones who lug the daytimers around with entries at half-hour intervals. Time is of the essence and is virtually seen as something that can be controlled. Certainly they believe they can run their lives. In group meetings, they are the first to ask about possible actions and who will be accountable and when.

Those who prefer perceiving like to explore all their options before coming to closure. They tend to see more choices and alternatives that need further exploration before decisions and plans are made. They are not stressed by what *J*'s would describe as "leaving things hanging." In fact, *P*'s often have numerous projects going on simultaneously. One of my *P* friends is still working on a rug she started four years ago. *P*'s *juggle* their priorities and *J*'s *set* theirs.

This scale accounts for much of the conflict we experience in our personal and professional lives. Participants begin to have a new-found appreciation for their children, spouses, and colleagues whose need to tie things up is genuinely and significantly different. The classic example we hear over and over is how families plan vacations. (This is where you can really separate the *P*'s from the *J*'s if you are having difficulty deciding your preference.) *J*'s want to have an itinerary specifying departure and arrival times, hotels, sites, etc. They usually have planned and coordinated their wardrobe and have even figured out on which day they will have to do laundry. A *P* doesn't need to have all of the specifics written out. What *P*'s want is a destination; when they leave and when they arrive are negotiable (unless they are flying). What they will do can be decided "in the moment" because they don't want to exclude possibilities sooner than necessary. They are therefore open to the new and emerging. They may pack at the last minute, forget their dress shoes, and have only three days of underwear for a ten-day trip,

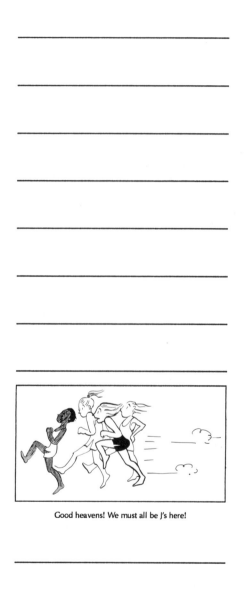

Good heavens! We must all be J's here!

but they'll solve these "problems" when they get to them. Laced with seriousness and laughter, the discussions and stories we share about these differences help to clarify and enlighten. The laughter comes from self-insight and is not derisive or blaming.

The MBTI seems to free people to be themselves. In appreciating their own diversity, they can begin to appreciate others. Underlying this session and all of our work is the importance we place on valuing our diversity. The MBTI is only one of many tools we give participants to accomplish this. It is an important way to begin the process of self-assessment within the context of community. The simultaneous assessment and development of the self with the community is the power of the training. Participants learn that empowerment of self is necessary to serve and empower others. The development of self should enhance community, and the building of community should enhance the individuals within it.

Questions for Reflection
1. How can you develop a better appreciation of yourself and your unique ways of learning and making decisions?
2. How can you develop a better appreciation and respect for others who are different?
3. How can you use your knowledge of self and others to be more effective in a leadership role?

She's really into Myers Briggs, isn't she?

LIVING INTO CONGRUITY

Claire Woodley

When you possess inner and outer balance, when what you feel and think inside match up with what you express to others, you have congruity in your life. Fully acknowledging, accepting, and rejoicing in who you are—and being that person for yourself and others—is basic in a spirituality that supports a congruent leadership style. Congruity is essential to honesty and integrity, both of which are primary aspects of healing and powerful leadership.

In my own spiritual journey, congruity has been a key issue. Being part of the leadership training team and participating in the training sessions have challenged me to a deeper relationship with all of who I am. It is my story of coming home to myself.

On the maiden voyage of the leadership training program in Monterey, California, I took an inventory exercise for the Myers-Briggs Type Indicator (MBTI). In the previous two years, I had undergone a career change from being a comedic actress to working for the national Episcopal Church Center. As is often the case, my career move involved some personal changes and major events in my life. As I switched from a "secular" to a "church" job, I thought that a bit of a behavioral change was called for.

My former career had been more than a job: it had been an arena where I could let loose my imagination, creativity, sensitivity, and impulses (some of those impulses were not in my best interest). I was the stereotypical "wild girl." After making a career change, having some important life experiences, and entering therapy, I had thought I would be a quieter person. Spiritual growth for me was equated with silence and quietness. What I actually had in mind was the role model of the "quiet girl." I didn't want to be Scarlett O'Hara anymore; I wanted to be Melanie Hamilton—good, kind, sweet, generous, quiet Melanie.

When I took the MBTI, I was shocked and dismayed to discover that I am an extroverted type. I felt that I had somehow failed, that all my attempts to change my behavior to being more congruent with being a "church lady" had been for naught. Deep down inside I was still the wild girl—impetuous and irresponsible. I had absorbed the cultural disapproval of extroverted women, who are labeled brassy, loud, pushy. Instead of affirming the extroverted woman for being assertive and articulate, I could only see and reject the negative cultural stereotype.

I began to reflect on this in the support group during the leadership training. I asked myself, When do you feel most fully you? Then I began to see that being extroverted is simply a part of who I am. If I wanted my leadership to be its most powerful, I needed to enter into a process of reconciling and uniting my extroversion with a healthy self-acceptance. I also needed to disassociate cultural baggage from self-destructive impulses, to separate tendency from compulsion. In short, I had to find Claire, because I ain't no Melanie and I ain't no Scarlett—I'm me. None of us are stereotypes, but we do adopt stereotypical behaviors, and we can change these. Loving myself was the first step in changing my behaviors and in claiming my power.

Feeling the pain of my lack of self-love and my desire to hide behind a stereotype opened some unexpected doors. Later, it helped me face other realities obscured by stereotypical behavior—like my own racism in choosing stereotypes who just happened to be white women slaveholders. I had never thought about the power dynamics implicit in such choices. The road to self-awareness helps me to hear others' pain because I have heard my own. When I become "real," I can see another's reality because it no longer threatens to topple any unreal construction I may be clinging to.

Stereotypes are powerful; because of their commonness, we mistake them for the truth. They conceal the reality of each individual woman and what women are really like as a gender. Because stereotypes mystify us, they obscure our ability to see or realize our power. As Betty Friedan said in her book *The Feminine Mystique*, mystification is also a useful tool in dismissing women, as in the saying, "Women, go figure 'em!" In other words, women are not understandable, and their lives and, therefore, their issues are simply "beyond" male understanding. As a result, it is a means of maintaining a status quo of oppression by commission and omission. Mystification keeps us from experiencing authentic mystery, the mystery of human life—the interconnection of birth and death of all living and nonliving things, of female and male. Mystification obscures power; mystery reveals power.

Having access to all of yourself, offering your wounds for healing, and loving and accepting yourself is building inner congruity. When we accept who we are, we accept who others are. In this way we build authentic relationships—a sign of a healthy spirituality. There is immense power in association, in building relationships. This is especially true in the circular model of leadership, where each member is equally valued and more members mean more power. Congruity exists between members of a circle because there are no false barriers of worth, class, race, or gender. Members have freedom of association that is denied them in a pyramid structure of power. When we are congruent, we experience personal unity and place ourselves in relationship to the world instead of in opposition. When we are truly ourselves we have freedom of association. This is a just and lively spirituality.

Experiencing personal congruity has been a long struggle for me. As an actor, I could be anybody else with great authenticity, but I didn't have to be me. The "me" that I lived with was often fragmented, and I never believed I was interesting or of value. Instead, I spent a good deal of energy creating a persona I thought would be irresistible. This was, in fact, repugnant to anyone with an ounce of integrity. It took me a long time to figure that out, because the persona I had built was the epitome of what all American girls are supposed to want to be and look like. It was an acquisition of the symbols of power accorded to women in order to compete with one another: beauty, thinness, clothing.

The old adage—that your blessing is your curse and your curse, your blessing—was certainly apt for me. The false selves we adopt are often maladapted true selves, and they can lead us to our inner reality. But there is a price: it is putting ourselves into the process of healing, of uniting and accepting all of ourselves, the true and the false. In accepting and forgiving our false selves, they become part of the true self. Our curse is transformed into a blessing. The gap between our false and true selves is also the potential for congruity. For those severely wounded, this is a word of hope, for the healing journey can seem, like mine did, a very long and endless process. It can also seem frightening, for once we enter willingly into the healing process, it consumes everything that obstructs the way to wholeness. The burning fire of healing will ultimately take us to whatever it is that has been dis-unified within us, whatever it is about ourselves that we have made outcast.

When we have congruity in our lives, we bring together parts of ourselves that have been alienated from our self-awareness. We discover places in ourselves that once were lost but now are found, things we were blind to but now see (to paraphrase the old hymn "Amazing Grace"). The term *grace* is appropriate here, for in the healing that

33

brings our true and false selves together, there is often that moment of insight that comes from within and beyond ourselves—a moment of grace.

We see it in ourselves and others. Frequently, one woman's breakthrough will precipitate another's. In finding personal congruity, we often experience group congruity. Such experiences give birth to songs like "There's a Sweet, Sweet Spirit in This Place." We recognize the Spirit moving within and without; we have experiences of continuity and unity; we recognize God in our experience—healing, reconciling, and making what was broken, whole.

> A healing spirituality is the opposite of alienation. It's a passion for life, a feeling of connection, of being part of the life around you. Many people experience it in nature, watching the ocean roll in, looking out over a vast prairie . . . when you are truly intimate with another human being, when you are uplifted through singing, when you look at a child and feel wonder, you are in touch with something bigger than yourself. There is a life force that makes things grow . . . . There's a part of everything living that wants to become itself, the tadpole into a frog, the chrysalis into a butterfly, a damaged human being into a whole one. And that's spirituality: staying in touch with the part of you that wants to heal, to be healthy, integrated and fully alive . . . .[1]

In one training session, a participant took the MBTI and tested as an extrovert. A soft-spoken, retiring woman, she was shocked. As the week progressed, she shared more and more of her life, how first her family and then her husband had demanded that she be quiet, that she stand in the background and be compliant and, above all, controllable. There was alcoholism in the family and abuse. She shared her experience of life as unreal, of herself as unreal. In the supportive environment of the training session, she tried out extroverted behaviors that she had always "sat on." With tears and many sighs of relief she told us how she was finally beginning to feel like herself, how after years of behaving in ways that felt foreign but were expected of her, she was finally acting on her preferences. The experience was a profound one. She got angry—good and angry—and for the first time in her life she didn't direct it inward against herself. Instead, she used it to change a reality that had become intolerable for her. As the writers of *The Courage to Heal: A Guide for Women Survivors of Child Sexual Abuse* have stated, anger is the backbone of healing. For this woman, anger became a strength that pulled her forward and transformed her life from an imposed unreality to a chosen, self-determined reality congruent with who she knew herself to be.

But what happened after the training? How did this woman face her family, her husband? What did she do with this new self? For this woman, being congruent included leaving her husband and entering an Al-Anon program. She kept in touch with members of her support group from the training session and began to build a new life, starting with one small step. She is firmly on the road now, coming home to herself. "Focusing anger precisely . . . [and] away from yourself clears the way for self-acceptance, self-nurturance, and positive action in the world."[2]

The different components of the training on anger management, assertiveness, power, and spirituality presented an extraordinary process whereby this "ordinary" woman—a woman who lived in an all too common milieu of abuse—could begin to see a new way for herself. For all of us, it is good to remember that we are on a journey, and the journey itself, as black women's liberationist Nelle Morton has said, is our home. It can feel overwhelming, but it is also good to remember that "the little part of you that is already whole can lead the rest of you in the healing process."[3] Each step builds our capacity to heal, to become whole, to love ourselves and accept love of this self from others.

"With this love comes a feeling of belonging, a sense of safety, a deeper experience of faith in your capacity to heal. And this love is not people oriented. It is based on a relationship with yourself that no one can take away."[4] The sense of personal congruence comes from loving yourself. While other people's love can nurture you, it cannot replace the power to transform that only comes with self-love and acceptance.

My growth into congruity was tested when I made the decision to act upon my inner promptings and external experiences and to pursue a call to the priesthood. I had done a thorough feminist analysis of patriarchy, the power structures of the church, and the church's role in maintaining patriarchy. How does a nice feminist like me talk herself into joining an organization that is a prime factor in her own oppression? Did this call mean that I was basically a masochistic person? What force had led me to think I could maintain congruity between my own beliefs and what I thought I would be expected to say and do (oh horrors!) to survive in this godforsaken pit of patriarchy? In a word: God.

It seems so simplistic, but what came to me was that God would never have gifted me in such a glorious and abundant way if I was not supposed to use these gifts. Furthermore, the church is not synonymous with patriarchy; neither is reality. God has a world that is a living, breathing process of transformation. I was a part of that process; I was a part of the church; I was an agent of transformation. To know what I know and to be who I am and not challenge systems of oppression would have been incongruent.

To reach congruity, however, I had to travel a long, hard road of getting good and angry, of looking at the situation directly and not overlooking any warts, of being ruthlessly honest about what I was getting into. It meant chucking whatever "stained-glass" notions I had of the church. It meant not having any fun in church for a long time. It meant losing some relationships and gaining new ones. It meant confronting myself and others through the painful work of consciousness-raising. It meant being a real jerk sometimes and later apologizing to people I had hurt. It meant laughing until I thought my sides would split from the lunacy of the whole enterprise.

Challenging patriarchal church systems has been painful. I have seen people act against themselves countless times when they were seeking to maintain structures of exclusion because the idea of inclusion was too threatening and the changes too vast. They were unable to see the power they had already lost through exclusion or the power they could have claimed in transforming the structures of alienation into structures of grace. Incongruity is fearful and painful. And I am called to be present to that pain as a healer, a change-maker, a priest. Building up congruity in the world builds the opportunities for all of us to become more congruent. And yes, day by day, through weeks and years, I have seen some change in the world around me and in myself.

For many women, unifying our beliefs and our actions is finding out what we already know. Becoming who we are—feeling and acting fully alive—is healing. Using the experience of personal unity and congruity in our leadership brings healing into the wider world.

Healing, spirituality, congruity, and unity: they are all connected, part of the cosmic dance. By living into congruity, we grow into the way of wisdom that recognizes the divine in the eye of every sister. This is the road to becoming fully alive.

Questions for Reflection:

1. When you were growing up, what messages did you hear about what girls were supposed to be like? About what you were supposed to be like?
2. When you reached puberty, what messages did you receive about what girls were supposed to like in relation to boys? In relation to other girls?
3. Did you want to cut off, to repress, any part of yourself? If so, what was it? Did it have anything to do with gender stereotypes?
4. Fill in the blank: "If I could say or do anything that I have always wanted to do, it would be _____." What is the relationship between what you want to do and the parts of you that got cut off or suppressed?
5. Think about a healing experience you have had, one in which alienated things were reconciled. How did it happen? What about you was made whole? How can you reconcile yourself with whatever cut off or repressed part has just surfaced?
6. What is it that keeps you from matching up what you think and feel inside with what you do on the outside?

Notes

1. Ellen Bass and Laura Davis, *The Courage to Heal* (New York: Harper & Row, 1988).
2. Ibid., 132.
3. Ibid., 156.
4. Ibid., 159.

SHARING POWER

Linda L. Grenz

I joined the training in Oklahoma and continued to serve as the only ordained woman on the staff of trainers for all but one of the training sessions. While I did not wear a clerical collar or take a markedly different role from the other trainers, my being ordained did have an impact on the training. One of the contributions I felt I brought was modeling how someone in leadership could empower others by *not* exercising power herself.

Usually I was the staff person who worked with the worship committee. This was both because I was ordained and could contribute in that area *and* because I hated leading morning energizers and could get the other co-trainers to do all of them if I took the worship committee responsibility.

At each training event, staff led worship on the first night. After that, the worship life of the group was decided by a worship committee that met over breakfast. My role as staff person was to get the meeting going. I would set the perimeters; the group would plan and lead all worship, from grace before meals to major services. We could recruit and involve anyone else. I was there as a resource person and to negotiate schedule or expectation conflicts with the staff.

Having stated those ground rules, I would ask what group members thought they would like to do. After a moment of silence, someone generally stated that she felt there should be grace before meals. A couple of other women would agree. Then everyone would look at me, and I would be busy eating my breakfast. Silence. Finally, I'd look up and say, "Sounds as though you'd like to have grace before meals. How could that be organized?" And then I would return to eating. Silence. Slowly they would begin working out whether the grace would be sung or said and who would lead it.

More silence. I would ask, "Anything else someone feels they'd like to see happen?" Soon a discussion would emerge around doing morning or evening prayer and the eucharist. The type, number, and schedule of services would be discussed with several "check-ins" with me as to what was "OK." I always encouraged group members to decide whatever they wanted to do, given the time and place constraints. That settled, they would again turn expectantly to me. I continued eating busily! Eventually, I would suggest we start planning the next service. And then I would hear the inevitable question, "What do *you* want us to do?"

Now, I admit that after five years of seminary and ten years of parish ministry, it is very tempting to "help" the women design a powerful and effective liturgy, sharing all my knowledge and experience. It is hard not to jump in and start helping them when they are all sitting there looking expectant. But what they were doing was empowering me and disempowering themselves. Silently, they were saying, "You are the ordained expert, so you should take charge and tell us what to do."

That dynamic happens unconsciously, and it is very seductive. Most of us clergy like to "help people"—we enjoy being needed. And we do, in fact, have knowledge, gifts, skills, and responsibility to provide liturgical leadership. Unfortunately, many of us often choose to use those skills and provide that leadership in a way that leaves us with all the power. Choosing to lead in an empowering way is difficult and often not the way to win a popularity contest.

My experience at the Upper Peninsula (Michigan) training event demonstrated that quite clearly. After several days of the worship committee turning to me for answers and my turning the question back to them, we arrived at the "night out." (The training schedule has built into it one evening when participants are encouraged to go out for dinner, if possible—as long as the time spent is together in large or small groups. The norm is that no one "goes home," or "runs errands," but spends time building personal relationships.)

The worship committee had decided to have a 7:00 A.M. eucharist the following morning to celebrate the life and ministry of a woman who had been a leader in the Episcopal Church Women and had been close to most of those present. Her funeral was that week, and they wanted to remember her. Since the service had not yet been planned, the group approached me and suggested we spend the evening planning the service. I affirmed their idea, and then pointed out that I would not be able to be present because the staff would be away from the conference facility that evening. This particular evening came after several days and nights of intensive training, and the staff knew we needed a break in order to rejuvenate ourselves and finish the training with energy. It was also our night to "take temperatures" on how we were doing as a team and how each team member was feeling. Skipping that time together was not an option for me: it was too important both to my well-being and for the training.

All of the women were active, participating Episcopalians. I already knew they could find the lessons in the Prayer Book and that several of them were experienced lay readers. In fact, with the shortage of clergy and the existence of small rural churches in the Upper Peninsula, some of them regularly conducted services in the absence of a priest. I felt sure they could put together a liturgy, and I told them that. I suggested that they design a service and slip the worship outline under my bedroom door. If there was anything major I was uncomfortable about doing, we would negotiate it in the morning. Otherwise I would do whatever they told me.

The worship committee was decidedly *not* happy about this arrangement. In fact, I later learned that several participants had "roast Linda" for dinner that night! But since it was the only way they could get the eucharist they wanted, they worked out a liturgy and put it under my door.

It was, as I expected, very well designed, and I had no problems doing what they had planned for me. At 6:45 A.M. we met in the chapel. The group braced to hear my objections. When I voiced none, I think they did not quite know how to react.

Having seen that they had rearranged the chapel in a circle of chairs around the altar, I asked where I should sit for the service. One chair sat alone behind the altar separated by a substantial space on either side. Puzzled looks crossed their faces. "Don't you *have to* sit there?" asked one woman pointing to the solitary chair.

"I can if that's where *you want* me to sit," I replied. "But I don't *have to* sit there. I can sit anywhere in this circle. It's rather lonely up there, and I'm not leading this liturgy alone. All I'm doing is starting the service, reading the Gospel, and leading the eucharistic prayer. If we all sit in the circle, the leadership can flow from one to the other naturally."

They all liked the idea. The chairs were quickly rearranged to close the gaps, and we all took seats around the circle, agreeing to cue the next reader by catching her eye when each of us was finished with our part.

The liturgy flowed gracefully. The prayers, reading, and songs they had selected wove a prayerful, joyful thanksgiving in honor of their friend. It was one of those liturgies that "worked." Afterward, one of the participants who was not involved in the planning thanked me for the beautiful and meaningful service. I quickly pointed out that it had been entirely planned by the committee members. "That's right!" one of the planners chimed in. "She didn't have anything to do with it. We planned it ourselves!" she said proudly.

As we walked to breakfast together, this same committee member told me that she had been very angry with me. She thought that I was derelict in my duty as a priest and that I would change everything they had planned and do it *my way.* Now that it was over, she realized that they could, in fact, plan a liturgy. "We learned we could tell a priest what to do!" she said with glee.

As we later discovered, the experience proved to be a powerful "learning" for most of the women on the worship committee. They were used to having clergy tell them what to do. For many, it was the first time a priest *allowed them* to make decisions about liturgy and to tell the priest what they wanted her to do in the service. When I refused to take the power, they were empowered to discover their own gifts and to create their own liturgy—which is, after all, the "work of the *people.*"

That empowerment was very evident in the worship committee's subsequent work. The group's last task was to design the closing eucharist. As we sat down to breakfast that morning, the tenor of the group was changed. Gone was the hesitancy and the looking to me for approval. Ideas flowed; women decided to "risk" experimenting with different ways of doing liturgy. Two women found the powerful reading, "Rich Woman, Poor Woman" and wanted to use it. I was an active participant but now just one of the group—not the external authority figure. The closing liturgy was deeply meaningful. It was truly "the work of the people" that celebrated God's presence in our midst.

Lay people often give all of the power to clergy—the power of the office, the role of clergy, and their own power, too. That power is seductive. Without realizing what we are doing, we, as clergy, often take all of it. When we do that, we have allowed the laity to disempower themselves. The same dynamic occurs with most leaders. Often group members initially give the power to the leader; if the leader takes it all, group members remain disempowered.

The difficult part of this is that group members often *want* the leader to take all of the power and will even try to force her to take it. If she refuses to take it, she may find the group engaging in "counter-dependent" behavior, or "acting like kids." If she does not take the power, some group members will "grow up" and share their gifts and skills, take responsibilities, and share the power with the leader and each other. Others (and sometimes an entire group) will get angry and throw a temper tantrum. Like children, they may shout, "I hate you. You're mean and ugly, and I'm going to find a new mommy." They'll ask the leader to do things for them or ask her permission to do things. They may even threaten to "run away from home" (leave the church or group) if things do not go their way.

They are, in essence, asking the leader to be their mommy. I often find it helpful to translate the group's talk and behavior into a playground setting—taking their words and actions and imagining them spoken in a child's whine. You might be surprised at how often it exactly fits. The problem is that if the leader takes the mother role—settles conflicts, smooths things over, comforts the group members, makes their decisions, and does their work for them—then she helps them disempower themselves, and she has "gotten stuck" doing *all* the work! (This is why clergy and lay leaders often end up "burning out.")

I believe the role of the leader is to lead—to motivate, enable, facilitate, and empower—not to do the group's work. The painful part occurs when the group refuses to grow up, make decisions, and take responsibility for itself. A project or program that is important to you may fail, and the temptation will be to rush in and rescue it. The cost of doing that is both exhaustion and frustration for the leader and a pattern of disempowerment for the group. Often the most empowering thing to do is to say *no* to exercising power—to let the group fail and learn from that.

As a priest, I have learned, and continue to relearn, that I am not the savior of the Church—Christ is. I'm not Christ's only minister—we all are ministers. When I "do it all," I participate in the disempowerment of the laity. When I "do my part" I usually get anger, resistance, and criticism. But in most instances, I eventually see people empowering themselves and each other to do ministry. When that happens, God's Spirit empowers all of us to be the Church.

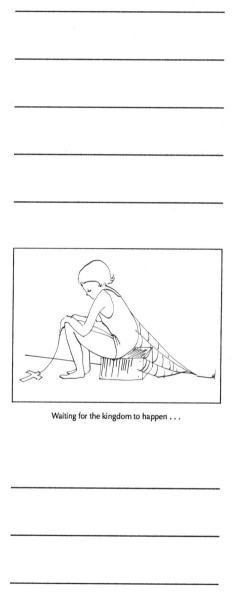

Waiting for the kingdom to happen . . .

THE IMPORTANCE OF BEING A MENTOR

Dorothy J. Brittain

It was the fall of 1985. The place was Sioux Falls, South Dakota, and I had been invited to join the WIMM leadership training team. I was pleased because I had heard from others throughout the Episcopal Church that this program offered good training for women. The training was planned to help women get hold of their lives, to become authors of their own lives . . . and I was definitely for that.

I was also surprised because, in my previous experience, "doing training" meant that I would be designing the activities. The activities in this leadership training, however, had already been designed. The task seemed simpler. All I had to do in South Dakota was be a member of a training team with three other women.

On this first training team, I worked with Ann Smith, Kathy Tyler Scott, and Pat Moore. This group of experienced trainers had, with Dee, designed the original program and had been the trainers throughout 1984. I was asked to join them at this and eventually other training sessions. (By the way, I was the first trainer added to the founding mothers.) It was for me the beginning of a learning, growing time. Once again I was reminded that an old dog can always learn new tricks.

I was aware that this team would allow me to find my own natural role and that they would accept this role as my contribution to the team. The design they had already made would prove flexible enough to make room for other trainers.

But I became aware that this training program was in several other ways new for me. Aside from occasional meetings in Chicago, this was the first time I had been in the Midwest. Here was a different culture. Cursillo, an international movement based upon prayer, study, and action, was a very important event for most participants. In fact, one morning a smiling group of women came into our rooms at 6:00 A.M. singing Cursillo hymns to awaken us. I was not amused. Most of these women also seemed to have been acculturated to a less affirming view of women that I was accustomed. I could not even locate on the radio dial my customary contact with the larger world, National Public Radio. However, as an experienced trainer I set aside my sense of dislocation and threw myself into the training program.

As we moved along through the program at Sioux Falls, I was aware that this training would challenge the emotions as well as the intellects of its participants. I immediately noticed that some women only told you who they were by naming their relationship to someone else—the rector's wife, the mother of so-and-so, a grandmother of many, the vice chairman of the local ECW. (Then, as now, I wish they had used the term *chairperson.*)

Later in the training, when she knew us better, a woman from South Dakota described herself as the storyteller of her people. This older woman took time to tell us the story of her native American tribe. Through her efforts and skills as a storyteller, we all became better informed, both about her people and about the values we share when we take time to tell our stories. When asked to talk about themselves, many women give shorthand role descriptions; they do not know that we will listen and seek to understand their story. Telling stories is another lesson in self-affirmation.

Although our short "lectures" were excellent, I learned that support groups are where much of the individual learning actually takes place. Without these groups, not much would happen for people who want to explore new thoughts and emotions, to exercise their right to try on a new behavior and receive feedback from others on how it works for them. To experiment and experience the new—to risk and grow—you need the support of a community, and this support must include both critique and affirmation.

I believe that encouraging openness and growth is an adult activity. This is especially important for women whose local culture and church have stereotyped them in their domestic roles or by their institutional, church-related affiliations. Women as well as men need to be known and appreciated for their God-given creative potential.

There were other significant "learnings," or insights, for me as well. On the training teams, we gradually realized that sexuality and spirituality were woven from the same fabric. One evening in front of the entire group, Ann and I engaged in a wonderful conversation about our own spirituality. Participants then had time to talk with others about their own spirituality. This seemed to work out well.

We were aware, however, that our design, or exercise, for discussing sexuality just did not work. In training, one learns never to use a design unless it has been tried out on the leadership team. This we did not fol-

'I am Mrs. DOCTOR John Jones (the eminent neurosurgeon), and Mother of the Vicar, the Rev. John Jones, Jr., and I have six GRANDCHILDREN. ALL BOYS, except one granddaughter named after me, Which is—uh. Which is—uh . . .'

low. We tried a new design in which a trainer's body was traced on newsprint and then the group was asked to call out words for different parts of the body. As I was watching the two trainers who were up front writing down the words, I could not help but notice that the design was falling apart. So was I! I could not stop laughing. I also wanted to cry. What did I do? I did not say, "Stop, this is not going well." No, instead I got on the floor in a fetal position. With a blanket draped over me, I tried to get away. I did not want to be in this picture, and the same was true for the participants. Given the participants' more conservative background, this design would never work. My attempts to hide—even escape—did not support the team. I had become childlike when things got out of hand. Such is the life of even an experienced trainer!

We became aware that sexuality and spirituality are part of who we are as humans. We cannot talk or think about one without the other in God's given time. As people with bodies, we are also spirit, and as spiritual people, we also have bodies. That is incarnation. Ann and I were being our sexual selves as we talked about our spirituality.

As a professional consultant, I am engaged to do educational and training events for a living, not as an avocation. I think that one of the particular gifts I bring to this vocation is an ability to help others name, claim, explore, and develop their theologies. Another way of saying this is that I help others look at their experiences and reflect on them in ways that clarify their understanding of God, themselves, and the world.

In doing this, I am a mentor. As trainers, we believe that mentoring is a particular way that women learn. Often, women want to acquire some new knowledge or skill, and a friend can help them accomplish this. The word *mentor* comes from ancient Greek and means "a guide to God." To us trainers, it means an experienced and trusted counselor.

Mentoring encompasses several components. The role is intellectually stimulating, serves as a model, inspires others to envision, and contains the tension of both challenge and nurture. Mentoring is often done by an individual, but a community can serve as a mentor as well. Knowledge is empowering, and mentoring is a way for us to be generous with this power.

Members of the training team mentor each other. As a group, we decide what we will learn in a particular community gathered for the training event. We work hard to make sure that our mentoring is collaborative instead of competitive. It should also allow individuals to try out new behaviors and receive feedback on them.

Both trainers and participants must face the same development tasks throughout their lives. It helps to find a soul sister (or brother) to support us in that task. As mentors, we assist in the development of our own and others' identity. Mentoring also helps us "know the ropes" of an institution.

In no small way, mentoring is responsible for the theological and personal growth that occurs among women in a short five-day training program. Although women often receive feedback about how supportive they are of others, it sometimes takes awhile for them to hear positive feedback about their own gifts, and strengths. Women may also be surprised to learn how important they are to one another in the process of exploration and self-discovery. The training not only teaches women to support others but to affirm themselves. The Body of Christ is decidedly interactive.

Before joining the leadership team, I worked mainly with men. From these experiences I learned a good deal about the exercise of power. Today I am convinced that, at this time in our history, women must learn to become more assertive, more in charge of their own lives, and better stewards of their own God-given power.

Through leadership training, many women discover clues or a clearer sense of direction about how they want to pursue the journey ahead. Many participants write or call to report that they are going back to school or taking a course. We can applaud this, celebrating those who find new ways to express their God-given gifts.

The training programs have taught me much about myself and about other women leaders in the church. For this I am grateful and pleased. If you want something done well, you should ask a woman to do it. If you want to bring about change in a creative way, ask women to take up the challenge. This is a part of the church's history and a part of women's lives today.

Questions for Reflection
1. Describe the circumstances when you began a sentence with the word *I* and did not feel embarrassed.
2. Describe how you became more self-confident. Who was with you? How did you feel?
3. Who has mentored you in your life? (Give names.) What did they do?
4. Whom have you mentored?

PLAYING FOR REAL: THE BLUES AND THE GREENS

Katherine Tyler Scott

A persistent challenge confronting the original leadership training team members was how we would respond to the issue of diversity. Given our norms of inclusivity and respect, it was obvious that, whatever we did, the end results would need to be a greater appreciation of differences and a celebration of our diversity. As women, we know what it is like to have our differences by virtue of gender denied and denigrated by the larger society. As a Black woman, I know the experience of being devalued solely on the basis of my skin color.

As we designed the training materials, we took the time to share and discuss our own stories. Predictably, these stories were peppered with vignettes of biases, prejudices, and racism. We recognized that who we were and how we perceived others had been shaped and formed by past experiences. We felt it was essential to share both the realities we faced and our "emotional baggage" so that our awareness could be used constructively. I am a firm believer that lack of self-awareness and insight is the basis for evildoing. In order to help other women deal with their racism and prejudices, we had to deal with our own first.

Many of my white friends complain to me about how they are treated in both secular, religious, church, and corporate systems. The word *invisible* comes up frequently. A common complaint is that ideas proffered by females are greeted with silence at best, put-downs at worst, only to resurface as "the brilliant idea of the day" when reintroduced by a white male. I had experienced this even more intensely.

In talking with the other trainers, I remembered a time when I was three years old. My father was in the Navy, and we were living in South Carolina. My twin sister and I went to the circus with our father, and we had an exciting and joyful day of balloons, clowns, elephants, trapeze artists, and cotton candy. We stood on the corner, the day now dusky, waiting for the bus to take us home. The bus finally arrived, and I lifted my short almond-colored legs up huge steps, took a few steps past the bus driver, and sat behind him. My father was putting coins in the token machine with my sister dutifully by his side. As he turned, he took her hand and walked down the aisle and told me to come with him. In my three-year-old mind I could see no reason for this. In the front, I had the best view, and there were plenty of empty seats. By the second time my father requested my presence, he was in the back of the bus, and the way he punctuated my name *"Katherine"* made me know that he was serious. Still, I thought I should be able to stay in my prime location where I could see so much more. Again, my father's voice invaded my thoughts, and this time the sternness and solemnity roused me from my seat. I knew by his words and the look on his face that I had to join him in the back of the bus. But true to my nature, I had to ask, "Why do I have to sit back here Daddy?" My father told me that I would get an answer at home. I will always remember that night. My parents explained to me that I was a special and wonderful person but that some people in this world would not be able to see me the way I am. They explained that sometimes these people could control what I could do, but they did not have control over my identity or my value as a person. This is a lesson I have carried with me through life and one that resurfaced to assist me in the leadership training program.

After doing several training sessions, we began to see a need for one of us on the training team to assume the responsibility for coordination. This person is called the lead trainer. This position included consulting with the diocesan planning group in preparation for the training event and, once we arrived on site, serving as liaison to the facility staff. We operated using the philosophy of *primus inter pares* (first among equals), in keeping with our circular, nonhierarchical view of organization and power.

When I have been the lead trainer, it has been difficult for the host institution staff to see me in this role. The dynamic that occurs is very much like the one my white friends bemoan when they are treated as if they are invisible. The staff of these institutions will frequently seek out white trainers to make decisions, adjustments, or to communicate information. Sometimes they would "look over" me and maintain eye contact with the other trainers. My assertiveness never failed me at such times, but what was difficult was observing and experiencing the collusive behavior of my team members, who cheerfully answered questions and made decisions. I could rationalize this to some extent. After all, we were all able, capable people, and no one was *the* boss. When patterns of communication and exclusionary behavior become fixed, however, it is a sign of an unhealthy system. And we knew that this was a clear violation of our norms. Our first response to such behavior was to go to the institution and reexplain how our team operated, reexplain the responsibility of the lead trainer, and rediscuss the relationship between the institution and this person's position. I discovered that rational, clear communication is no remedy for such forms of "–isms."

As we discovered again and again in our work with each other, we had to begin with *ourselves.* In this instance, it meant talking about what was occurring and how each of us behaved and felt. Through a willingness to return to self-exploration and a reexaminiation of our own beliefs and values, we could take responsibility for our own behavior and determine how we would change it. Reminding my colleagues that their perception of me as wonderful and competent was not shared by our host institution was in some cases a revelation! Once this was accepted, we could decide how to combat such behavior. We agreed that the trainers would stop responding to staff who persisted in coming to them but would assertively refer them to the appropriate person, especially if she were an African-American trainer. While we may not have changed institutional attitudes in any significant way, we changed ourselves and modeled what we said *we* believed and valued. The learnings, or deep insights, from this are rich indeed. There is tremendous power in naming what is going on, no matter how ugly it is. This is especially true if you claim the power you have to change the way you behave and respond. The struggle to live out our ethics and to be congruent with beliefs and behavior has served to strengthen and empower our training teams. It has not always been without pain and cost, however. We have learned that the extent to which we must deny "unacceptable" parts of ourselves is the extent to which we project these "unacceptables" on others and often end up scapegoating or excluding them. If we must deny our own feelings of rejection and low self-esteem, then we can easily displace these onto others who we can label as inferior, "one down," or not as good. Our self-esteem becomes predicated upon another person or group being lower in value. We minimize any opportunity for individual growth when we put this dynamic in place, and we nurture the opportunity for doing harm in such circumstances.

You can begin to see that a strong norm among the trainers is to work on self in preparation to train and serve others. When this is violated, a crisis occurs within the team much as it would if any important community norm were violated. We have lost two skilled trainers because of this. In both instances, we saw the trainer as having put herself in a position of being "one up" and unwilling and unable to look at the impact of this attitude and attendant behavior toward others.

Most of us have been exposed to racism and understand its impact on us and our daily work. To deny that we have biases, prejudices, and –isms is to unleash evil on the environment. A lack of awareness means that we act without full knowledge and are capable of doing great harm no matter how admirable our intentions are to do good. It means that we can rationalize and justify behavior that is harmful to others. It means we live in a state of denial and incongruity, our stated beliefs inconsistent with our actions. But worst of all, it means that we can perpetrate the oppression of others while couching our behavior in virtuous terms. As a training team, we expect that we must practice what we preach and model what we expect others to learn and become. As mirrors and mentors to a community, we must engage in ongoing self-examination and change.

Our learnings have come from our relationships and experiences with each other and the communities with which we have worked. (Powerful learnings have come from our experiences of pain and brokenness.) In our first two training sessions, we felt challenged about how we could best facilitate an examination of biases, prejudices, and –isms. Our efforts in this regard have really chronicled our growth as trainers. Initially, we tried a design that unfortunately reinforced intellectualization, denial, and flight. We discussed the meanings of biases, prejudices, and –isms. In small groups, we shared our answers to questions about our own history and past exposure to prejudice. It sometimes amazes me how we all can forget what we know. For example, we know that learning must be experientially based and grounded in the here-and-now. As soon as we observed how participants ran from these hard issues, our memories quickly returned. We knew that if we could not move these issues from the head into the heart, then the –isms in our church would likely remain shrouded in a nice Christian vocabulary of denial and piety.

In our second training session, we include an allegorical film entitled *The Silver Stream*. Through the metaphorical messages, participants felt somewhat safer exploring their experiences, feelings, and attitudes. The level of denial and flight, however, remained uncomfortably high. Participants would say things like, "I grew up in or I live in an all-white community—we don't have a problem with racism," or "I don't see color; you're a person just like me." And these would be said with everything from indignation to warm, loving innocence (all forms of resistance to self-exploration). Although we felt pleased with the changes in this section of the training program, we knew that more improvements were needed.

In a moment of quiet reflection at home (in between training events), it occurred to me that what we needed was a shared here-and-now experience within community that would provide a basis for reflective learning. I created a simulation game called "The Blues and the Greens." In this game, participants are placed in small groups, and each is assigned roles they are not to tell anyone else about. All of the assigned roles have equal ability and skill, but some are "up" (powerful) and some are "down" (powerless). The group's task is to create a plan for the ideal church community. The process is inherently incongruent with the task, for it places participants in a position of trying to accomplish something they are not living out. After the game is over, there is a process of discovering powerful insights into our behavior. This game is so powerful that the game time was reduced from forty-five to thirty minutes. We believe this is because the process really parallels our real lives—what most women and minorities experience daily.

Our society has adapted to the pyramid model of power and its exclusionary system with some serious consequences. One participant discovered how easy it is for her to be passive and deny being excluded as a way to retain some sense of human dignity. She also discovered the Catch-22 this placed her in: to be a part of an oppressive system, she accommodated it. As a result, she compromised her beliefs, lost her identity, and eroded her self-esteem. No wonder she felt anxious and alienated. Incredible insights from thirty minutes!

Other participants found that power is also an aphrodisiac and that there is a thrill in being at the top of the pyramid. But in reflecting upon their experience, they were able to see the "down side" of being "one up." In the pyramid structure, a leader must always appear to be all-knowing and competent. The leader directs and decides without a comprehensive knowledge of the followers' needs. And even when a sector of voices within the group cannot be heard, the leader operates as if she has complete information. Such a leadership position is lonely, isolating, and, in the long term, debilitating. The leader can easily become overextended and overworked. Such leaders frequently complain that "no one will help." And in truth this becomes a self-fulfilling prophecy. Those who work under such leadership do become "inept" and less dependable.

Some women in the training events balked at having to "go through the Blues and Greens." "I would never behave like this in a real-life situation!" they would say, either apologetically or angrily. "Couldn't we just affirm and celebrate our differences without having to do this?" is a question I have heard a few times. Our response to such questions is to help participants see the similarities between "the game" and real life. In the training, they can leave their roles after thirty minutes; minority women live with this kind of process continually. White women also contend with similar dynamics because of gender. What "The Blues and the Greens" does is sensitize us to the impact that exclusion and brokenness have on a community. It exposes the pyramid model of power as one that usually creates an unhealthy community in which no one is spared. It takes tremendous energy to keep another human being "down" as the basis for your staying "up." It is incredibly draining to figure out how to manipulate the people with power into doing what you want. We all lose. Some of us are more immediate and visible victims of such a process, but we are victims nevertheless—unless we decide to transform the pyramid into a circular model of shared power. We can choose to see power as unlimited rather than finite. We can share power and empower others. We can choose to be conscious of how we exclude some and include others and how we inadvertently diminish the contributions of those whose involvement could ultimately enrich our work, the church, and the larger society. We can decide to value the contributions and gifts of others.

For white women, this may mean claiming that they live in dual roles. As women, they experience being "downs." As whites, they are perceived as "ups." When they can claim their "upness," they can begin to cease colluding with an oppressive system. The claiming of this "upness" must be done without the accompaniment of chronic guilt. Guilt can be so debilitating, and it is a wonderful excuse for doing nothing. Feeling overwhelmed by issues can be an excuse for inaction, a form of maintaining the status quo. As "downs," they must reject the idea that they are inferior. Their experience should help sensitize them to the experiences of minorities and make them more determined to seek a just and caring society for all.

For African-American women and other minorities, having their contributions valued means claiming the power to define themselves regardless of others' perceptions. As Eleanor Roosevelt put it, "No one has the power to make you feel inferior without your consent" (the lesson I learned at age three). I know what a challenge this can be, for I have taken periodic vacations from calling people on their negativistic behavior. Yet, as humanists and Christians, we are called to do this.

I have had to decide where best to use myself in this regard. I could spend my whole life dealing with every –ism and –ist, but this would be a waste of my time. I have gifts and talents to use in other ways—we all do—and they don't absolve me of the responsibility I have for doing something to alleviate injustice and suffering. I believe I will be forgiven for having an occasional respite from vigilance and action against the –ists and –isms, as long as I remember that it is a permanent job I share with others. Failure to point out the –isms perpetuates them and poisons community.

As trainers, we have experienced how difficult it is to change behavior. In conducting "The Blues and the Greens," we ran into resistance among ourselves when some of the white trainers gave participants "mixed messages" about the choices they had in the simulation. Once a person was in role, they were to stay in that role; I didn't want them to have a choice about this. There *was* a choice in the way the role was carried out. Through it all, we had to again confront our own attitudes and feelings. Because –isms are painful, we feel pain in confronting them. Only when we face our brokenness do we have a chance to heal and bring about wholeness.

After one particular training session during which we had conducted "The Blues and the Greens," we had the usual mix of feelings about the experience. Most participants sensed a change in attitude. But others resisted the notion that the –isms were a problem at all. Interestingly, this community involved a greater than usual number of African-American women. While the Caucasian women said that they saw no problem in their diocese, the African-American women were silent, giving no indication verbally or nonverbally that they disagreed. Obviously, they did *not* want to pursue the subject.

In a later session on group process and development which Edna Brown and I facilitated, we asked this community of women to form four small groups of nine members each. In the larger body, they sat black and white intermingled. When the groups were formed, however, we ended up with one all-black group, one all-white group, one integrated group, and one group with one black woman. In the process of forming these groups, we had observed that the all-white group had started with one black member. But when a white participant came up, it was the black woman who left so that the groups would have equal numbers.

We decided to share with the group the behavior and results we had observed. Edna began sharing our observations, since she was facilitating this portion. The barrage of hostility and denial that resulted was incredible. The trainers were accused of "creating problems": we were bringing racism to an otherwise inclusive, harmonious, and diverse group! The groups' inability to own their behavior and the underlying feelings and attitudes led to massive projection onto the trainers. To us, it smacked of "killing the messenger," but we kept working to heal the rift that was now inalterably exposed. The fact that two black trainers facilitated this process may have added to the community's inability to become unstuck. The two white trainers were silent throughout the initial exchanges and, in fact, sat in the back of the room physically detached until the very end. That night in our standard training team processing, we again talked about our own behavior and attitudes. Our white colleagues had another opportunity to confront their own racism (as well as their discomfort with conflict of this magnitude). I have a penchant for truth-telling, and this experience reminded me of how dangerous it can be to point out opportunities for learning that others are not ready to have. The incongruity between actions and stated beliefs was blatant, and saying so had unleashed emotions so powerful that denial and attack seemed the only options for this community. We felt what we did was ethical and right, but we ached over the pain and brokenness confronting us.

The next day, our last, was to be one of closure, ending with a celebration of the eucharist. Linda, a priest and one of the training team members, was going to be the celebrant, having worked with the community's worship committee to plan the service. How, I wondered, were we going to deal with the pain in this community, with the incongruity between words and behavior, with the evil I saw in the guise of scapegoating and denial?

As I stood that morning to begin our work, I realized that the design in the notebook would have to be put aside. We could not deny our experience, our life together, and gloss over the pain and brokenness. Just the evening before, several women had been cutting out paper dolls of various colors to drape across the altar. These dolls were to symbolize community and diversity. One of the women who was African-American picked up some black and brown paper and began to cut. A white woman said, "We're not using those colors; we want to use the bright, pretty ones!" At the time the African-American woman said nothing. She ceased to form the dolls. She ceased to form herself. During the night she awoke and realized what had happened. "The Blues and the Greens" was not a game to her. It was reality. In the morning, she dressed and went to the altar. She sat and cut dolls from brown and black and added them to the garland surrounding the chalice and bread. She felt a rush of energy and bubbled over as she shared her insights and actions with one of the trainers.

Conscious of all this, I looked out over the faces of the women, recalling all that we had experienced. I began to share my feelings about what had happened the previous day. I began with the statement, "I must be congruent." Tearfully, I shared my sadness, pain, and sense of separation. Unless we could face our brokenness, I did not feel I could participate in the eucharist if it was viewed as a way of glossing over our differences. This led to more sharing of thoughts and feelings, which was greatly needed. There was no resolution. The silent African-American woman began to speak, although it was still evident that to go so far as to speak the truth would exact too high price—a price the community was not prepared to pay.

What was achieved was a recognition of the reality of our experience and an acceptance that we were not in unity. I left this community with the hope that we had moved from being scapegoats to being catalysts for further individual exploration for more of the women. Perhaps we left nothing of any lasting value. As a team, we were ready to accept this option. I was reminded of how we can withstand incredible adversity when we are bonded to others who share a belief in mutual respect. I had once again found power in being congruent and in being in community.

Questions For Reflection
1. What was your first experience of being treated differently because of your gender or race?
2. How do you feel around others who are different from you?
3. What do you need to do to increase your comfort with and respect for those of a different race?

MARY DOESN'T LIVE HERE ANYMORE

Eleanor Smith

It was my good fortune to be included in the creation of this book. Being an illustrator is something I like better than anything in the world. It is probably antithetic to my training as a journalist and my experience in commercial advertising. But in the days when I was serving as the token woman on the vestry, washing my share of parish dishes, observing the pecking order rituals amid the male hierarchy conducting diocesan business, and serving on consecutive triennial planning boards, cartoons were my safety valve. Originally private, then shared with friends on the same wavelength, these small observations in india ink began to turn up in sacristies and offices and then in publications. They were one woman's humor, of course—my humor. But more and more often I found that a cartoon observation spoke for many other women in the church. I also learned that, for a surprising number of people, humor and religion do not mix well, humor being suspect, disrespectful, even threatening. I have heard from these people, too. But for the most part, readers have said that my cartoons fill a certain void, that they illustrate a common predicament. The cartoons help people feel they are not out there alone.

Besides serving as this book's illustrator, I was also a participant in the training. In fact, I was a *result*. I had emerged at the far end of five intensive days convinced, affirmed, and set on course. I had been a lone woman sitting in a pew at St. Apathy's, wondering why I felt so isolated, why Martha was always portrayed as a shrew (when later Gospels indicate otherwise) and Mary was portrayed as the male ideal of female submissiveness. Then it dawned on me that many women are in many St. Apathy's. These are women whose gifts and talents have been kept in boxes, unused, whose voices have not always been heard or whose outlets for service have been confined to the parallel church of women's organizations. With all my heart, I hope these women will have the opportunity to take leadership training, whether it is the excellent training described in these pages or its sister program, the Women of Vision training sponsored by the national Episcopal Church Women (ECW). I believe that the church will recognize the tremendous

She sleeps
locked into her space. Not unhappily. Just static. Confined.

untapped potential of its women, but that the women themselves must first take up their responsibilities to God and to themselves.

I experienced leadership training in 1986. A cancellation in one diocese made it available suddenly in mine. The planning was characterized by an intense organizational effort and a supportive letter from our supportive bishop. Forty of us—some from other dioceses and provinces—gathered to take part. We were older women, younger women, African-American women, Hispanic women, women I might never have met, ordained women, native American women, well-known women, working women, women wearing clothes other women would kill for, women in blue jeans—Episcopalians all.

I knew why I was there, or so I thought. But looking around me, I had a profound insight, or learning. For the most part, these other participants had been untapped by the church or "side-trapped" in the outer hallways of the church's labyrinthine structuring. Some had never participated in the ECW, Daughters of the King, Cursillo, or any other organization. But all were present to seek actively a new direction for their journeying. They came to be affirmed.

The women I knew well had reasons for enrolling much the same as my own. We wanted spiritually based training in order to do our work in the church better than we had been doing it. We wanted to release the flow of energy we knew was there.

As a laywoman working in the world of male clergy and high-powered male executives, I had learned by experience what worked and what did not. Over the years, I had compiled my own list of who worked and who did not. I had come up through the ranks of the ECW, parish to diocese to province, as one job opened into the next without thought or goal for self. My election to the council of the diocese was a sort of zany apocalyptic affair. I was not present at the convention when my name was placed in nomination. I had not even been consulted. And I won—handily, they say. Thus I became that year's token woman on the council. I was either "Miss Eleanor-ed," pampered and *then* ignored, or just plain ignored. I take that back. At my very first meeting, a priest (now a bishop, incidentally) and a prominent layman quizzed me on the state of my *morals*.

However, I found my place, especially after a new diocesan bishop was elected and consecrated.

As you may know, a curious ambience surrounds a new diocesan bishop. During this time of corporate ambivalence, I learned to expect

And then
something new intrudes. Its tiny roots intrude and she becomes aware . . . there is something else out there! Growing!

a whisper behind me saying, "Ask him what he intends to do about this and that." If I turned around, the person behind me would be adjusting a shoelace. After I asked the question, the council would be informed—because a gentleman accords a lady seeking information clearly detailed statements, lest she misunderstand. I would then muse about whether this was seen as my primary value, to be the one to ask the "dumb" question. That way, if they truly turned out to be dumb or irritating, my status did not count. I was a laywoman.

Occasionally, the council would turn as a body and ask, "What do the women think?" I would then attempt to speak on behalf of every woman in the diocese, of every diverse opinion, theology, and color. But it seemed clear to me that the council was not interested in what women thought, but in whether "the women" would support whatever they were planning.

I am thankful this has changed. Women have been seated on, elected, and/or appointed to diocesan councils and committees. Women are making themselves heard and noticed, their gifts of decision-making and leadership are being used, and their experience accumulated through years of hands-on service in the parallel church is being put to good use. There is still more work to be done, however.

As chair of various committees and departments, I have presided over both men and women and have puzzled over how often I am cast as "Mother." It seems to be a peculiarly female problem. Mother will understand if a report is not on time (the excuse usually being automotive, if a male, or gynecological, if a female). Mother will soothe and understand and extend the due date. A gender game. I had not realized until the training how I, too, had fallen into this mode, saying, for example, of Supreme Court Justice Sandra Day O'Connor, "But she's a *woman*! How can she rule against her own sex?"

Women perceive leadership differently; our gender gives it different twists and expectations. Working in the world of male clergy, I could not help but notice the differences. For instance, as a leader I never had a harem of eager volunteers to take the minutes, do the copying, or write the letters. At one meeting, I actually did all these things plus prepared the lunch, stopped the meeting at noon to serve and clean up before resuming the meeting. I do not regret or resent any of this. I merely felt that somewhere, somehow, there must be a better way of exercising leadership—my leadership.

I had come to the training event with this history. Among the partici-

Awakening, tentatively she explores.
Not yet ready to leave her broken shell, her old security, she begins to take in the essence of the new.

pants gathered was a young woman who had given me one of my most valuable learnings in church-related work, in community service, or even in recreation. I had been asking people what fee they would consider reasonable for a certain course. This woman said that she had an invisible cut-off figure of what she could spend on herself. A dollar over that figure and she would be depriving her family. The guilt, she said, was not worth it. My surprised "Aha!" was one of recognition. It also was one of the givens for our present gathering, because each woman there had written a check representing a choice, had carved out the time, had chosen among other obligations, and had driven many miles to be present—all because her need overrode any of those things. We were forty women clutching the thick, white training manuals we had little time to digest, eyeing each other.

Until
freed, she leaves the old way behind.

There was an older woman, widowed, and a younger woman, recently widowed: Were their needs the same? Could I possibly understand? There was an overweight woman with a pretty face and an "I'm-not-sure-I'll-like-this" diffidence. Was this gathering meant to be five days of bashing men? Being touchy-feely witnesses? What *kind* of spirituality were they talking about? Was the woman priest going to be divisive in our traditional diocese just by being present? Would we be changed beyond recognition by the time this was over?

The consultants were friendly but remote and professional. There was beautiful brown Kathy Tyler Scott (I say brown because she taught me that black meant sixty-eight different shades); clean-cut, blue-eyed Ann Smith, who looked fourteen years old most of the time; gorgeous, former model Pat Moore of the lavender eyeliner and cool British accent; and Linda Grenz, present as a consultant with the team for the first time, given to machine-gun delivery and ricochet laughter.

Our first task was to create name tags out of construction paper and bits of color. Not many like to do this, but it was a way of defining ourselves for others, with often fascinating results. I concocted a straightforward *E*—honest but not revealing. As the days went on I wanted to change mine. What had I purposely kept back and private? I was learning.

We were put into small groups with one trainer. Our group drew Kathy Tyler Scott. Whether it was Kathy's great skill as a trainer or the makeup of the group, I cannot say. But we bonded almost at once. We told our stories and were caught up in each other's unfolding dramas. We role-played a bittersweet scene between mother and daughter and a hilarious confrontation between a frustrated vestry woman and a wildly macho senior warden. We screamed with laughter and recognition; we hugged; we wept quietly in the sympathy of sisters.

In plenary and during assignments, other stories surfaced. A fragile young Hispanic woman caught in a chauvinist culture emerged as shining steel. The pretty but overweight woman, trying to balance on the periphery of the training, finally faced up to the fact that she was hiding, barricaded by flesh. The older woman accepted her sexuality. Through the laughter and the love, she came alive in her own eyes—a powerhouse of a woman who had much to give in all components of her being.

Now and then, as our paths have crossed in the intervening years, I have learned of the next chapters of these women's lives and how the training had influenced their decisions. I recall a young woman in a bullying situation who stood by her convictions publically—a no-win situation to many onlookers but a victory for her because she had cleared her role in it. Another woman accepted the leadership of a large diocesan organization with every confidence she would succeed—and she has. "The training was the turning point in my life," she told me.

Through the training, I sensed the unnamed theories around me—but whose? How could these four trainers scatter such mind-boggling concepts—freedom and servanthood as joy not slavery; responsibility to self for growth; sexuality paired with spirituality—with such ease and assurance? A college graduate with some postgraduate work, I felt semi-informed, nearly illiterate. As a participant, rather than a leader, I was *in* a body of established theory. To grow as fast as I could, I had to overlook the mechanics in order to ingest as much as possible in the five days. Growing pains at age fifty-plus can feel very odd indeed. I once did a cartoon of a woman on a trapeze and having to let go and reach for the hands of her catcher. The risk summed up, for me, what was going on. I was experiencing my own growth. Every woman there was unique and possessed gifts the rest of us did not. Together we formed a whole. Each of us was needed to make that whole. To attain this wholeness, I had to be fully present. It had nothing to do with the fact that some had remarkable talents and others seemingly were short-changed. We all fit together.

The Myers-Briggs personality testing clarified much for me. As a conceptualizer, I finally understood the isolation I felt when others were unable to see what I saw so clearly. For example, when I was the token

But more!

_____

_____

_____

_____

_____

_____

woman on the parish vestry, my suggestions were regularly rejected out of hand. Minutes later, one of the men would present the same idea as his solution, and it would be accepted with acclaim. I finally learned that a conceptualizer must not give the solution without having led others to it by a carefully constructed path. Such lessons in patience must surely build character. I still do not always remember to do this, but at least I now know the corrective.

I observed other marvelous behavioral insights. At one point, we were grouped by our MBTI identities and given raisins. When each group reported back, we learned that one group had analyzed those raisins, counted them, and produced a sheet of data. Another group had turned them into a design. Another based a health and nutritive example on them. And the intuitive group reported cheerfully, "We didn't do anything. We *ate* them."

The only part of the training I had difficulty with was the "Blues and the Greens" game. I hated it. One reason the game was so difficult was that I am known as a "fixer." To be caught in a role where my brilliant solutions were totally ignored was infuriating, especially since I did not know why I was being ignored until the end of the game. It still smarts, this learning. But at least I am aware of the uglier group dynamics that can happen, and I know what to do.

She shares with another who is now as she once was.

Throughout the five days, self-discoveries seemed to assault our senses. My roommate told of appreciating, for the first time, the strong and gifted women in her family who had gone before her, shaping her, mentoring her.

For some participants, the presence of a woman priest in their lives was a watershed. Their initial anxiety had arisen, in part, because they were unsure of how to act. They had arrived ringed by "oughts" that dissolved as they worked together and with Linda Grenz, the staff's ordained member.

For myself, I made strides toward accepting my gifts. I had become so used to denigrating my gifts, denying them, or simply trying to diffuse them.

I am now also owning up to my own opinions. As chair, I have always tried to give others free reign to ventilate their ideas, but as a woman I am also claiming my own right to speak. This has been remarkably freeing for me. It is as if I have at long last dropped the baggage of adolescence, those days when "everybody" owned a red convertible or stayed out until 1:00 A.M. "Everybody" had even accompanied me into my marriage to dictate how I arranged my furniture and raised my children.

That the training was an intense experience is an understatement. The last night, we broke free in an explosion of spirits, sometimes dancing on tabletops. We did wonderful take-offs on our teachers. Who will forget Ann Smith as an aging bag lady in the care of a nurse? (I can't, because I did the skit.) or the grinning Toothless Fairy? or any of the other improvisations? We laughed until we were helpless for we were with sisters, and with sisters one can risk. It sounds funny, I know, but with sisters one can even risk living the gospel at St. Apathy's. The Martha and Mary story stands for both diversity and for Jesus' acceptance and his inclusion of both women.

The next morning we gathered in the chapel for the eucharist, celebrated by our own woman priest/consultant/trainer/friend. She preached a homily about brokenness and wholeness, about how the past five days had brought us to the recognition of our brokenness, and about how we could now take our broken pieces to God and ask for healing. She gathered us around the altar, laying healing hands on our bowed heads. For many that last day, the connection was made that the *eucharist* binds us together. The *eucharist* transcends the boundaries of proscribing thought about who shall or shall not celebrate. The *eucharist* is important and has the power. The bread and wine and the healing came from Jesus' hands. The discoveries and the tensions, the joys and the exhaustion melded into a healing that was complete. We were released back into our lives and work as whole beings.

I have continued to gather "Aha's"—moments of insight—now that I know what to look for and what I need to work on in my own development. The training has given me the opportunity to return the gifts God intended me to use in God's service. That, to me, is my wholeness.

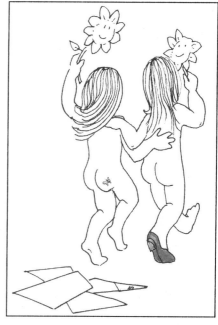

The same awakening occurs.
They affirm each other.

CLAIMING OUR SEXUALITY AND SPIRITUALITY

Claire Woodley

My arrival on the leadership training team began suddenly one summer afternoon. I was working in a battered women's shelter as part of my seminary training and had called Ann Smith to ask some questions and catch up. When I was still working as Ann's assistant in the WIMM office, we had talked about my joining the leadership training team as an apprentice after my graduation. But Providence would not wait that long. The day after our phone conversation, I was on a plane to Milwaukee doing my first stint as a leadership trainer-in-training. Baptism by fire!

During my years in the WIMM office, I had worked with the original training team to put together the nuts and bolts of the program. Later, I had been a participant at the first training event. It was a life-changing occasion that made me take seriously a vocational call to the priesthood. The training gave me the tools with which to live and thrive in the church while I participated in feminist critique and worked for change. Perhaps the greatest tool was learning to use anger as a creative power and not as a rageful, wasting one. This was no small feat! That first training event was a gateway for me, and now I was going through another passage, my first time as a trainer-in-training.

I had the expected fears and reservations. Would people know that I had been "just" the secretary at the WIMM office? Would they accept my leadership? Would my age be a problem? Would I be able to remember all the training material and be able to communicate it intelligibly? The really big plus I had going for me was that I had worked with the other women on the training team for a number of years. All of them had been mentors to me. Each had given me some special gift that enlarged my own. Above all, they had never related to me hierarchically. My participation on the team as secretarial support had always been valued and no one had ever felt the need to limit my contributions on the basis that I had been *only* a secretary. My work with the women's office had been my first experience of a feminist model that valued personhood and the unique contributions that each person could make. More than anything else, this experience showed me what church could be. I had experienced God as freedom, but I needed a corresponding sense of church.

In the leadership process, in the supportive communities of the training sessions, in giving and receiving feedback, I came into an understanding of myself as a valued friend, teacher, thinker, and contributor. With the support and commitment of the people in this process, I made great strides in the making of who I am. By this I mean the growth that happens when relationships strive to be as open and honest as possible and have as their ideal mutual nurturing and learning between peers. This growth honestly assesses areas we need to work on, and honestly works toward changing behaviors and patterns that keep us stuck. Such was the community that developed during the training event.

The transformation that takes place in the leadership training communities is a deeply spiritual experience. I have been, and continue to be, awed by the creation story as it continues to unfold in the lives of the women who claim their leadership and walk in the power that is their divine gift.

When my plane landed in Milwaukee, I was tuned like a radio receiver, picking up all the signals and looking for patterns. I could not wait to see what God and the women would do together in the coming week.

When we arrived at the conference center, I was struck by its rigid institutionalism. There were long granite corridors and bare rooms with a bed and a sink. Every object, wall or floor, was a uniform gray, brown, or beige. The building itself was enormous and surrounded by acres of lawn, with no chairs or trees or walks. The grounds and the building seemed to be objects that existed by themselves, for themselves. There was little or nothing human about this institutional building: it seemed to reject flesh and blood. Climate, food, space, direction, and administration were all strictly controlled.

When we sought out a friendly cup of tea to begin our meeting, we were told that under no circumstances were we to enter the kitchen or speak to the people who worked there. We were to channel all requests through an office on the other side of the building, about a three-block walk away. Built to train young men for the Roman Catholic priesthood, the long corridors and sterile rooms echoed with a vast silence and emptiness. Lacking men with vocations, the Roman Catholic diocese had opted to make this architectural dinosaur into a retreat center.

The challenge of building a community of trust and growth in such a setting was formidable. As we worked together, catching up on the new learnings and events in each other's lives, we began to make decisions about who would present each section of the training.

Since its inception, the leadership training program had struggled to articulate the team's evolving sense of spirituality and sexuality and to translate this into a viable experiential learning. We decided to utilize my seminary training, my feminist analytical skills, and my experience as a dancer and actor to present the section on sexuality and spirituality.

For the training team, just speaking about spirituality itself had proven difficult. We were much clearer on how to speak about feminine sexuality than feminine spirituality. We realized that we could not talk about spirituality as an entity separate from the rest of our lives, loves, and work. It is not a product. Rather, spirituality is the personal state of being from which all behavior flows. Spirituality is seen through relationships to people, God, and all of creation. Our psychic health, religious understanding, and sexuality all intersect in our spirituality and affect its development. When these parts of our lives are in harmony, we are spiritually healthy. In order to address spirituality in the training, we needed to address the various aspects of life and to teach skills that help us work toward harmony with ourselves and with others.

Another facet of our understanding of spirituality is the importance of lived experience and learning from another. This is an old and venerable spiritual tradition. For centuries, when one chose or was called to undertake the religious life, either formally or informally, people spent significant portions of time with holy people learning how they *lived.* Their lives were the testimony to their spiritual growth. In our living with one another for those five days, short as they are, we learn a great deal as we see one another struggle through barriers—in training sessions, small groups, celebrating, nights out, and those cherished late night talks that swell into tears and laughter. We grow spiritually in our living together because we are in concrete relationships with others.

Initial efforts to present a spirituality section had been problematic. The first obstacle was religious sloganeering. "I'm a born-again Christian" or "Jesus loves me and that makes it all OK!" were two of the most popular. We found that the sloganeering proved to be "stoppers." Stoppers are statements based on untested assumptions used to stop conversation, elicit a compliant response, or keep conversations and relationships on a superficial level. The veracity of the statement's content is not in question; it is how the statement is used that is suspect.

The statements themselves are generalizations that prevent community from happening. Stoppers are ideological and not experiential. They do not facilitate spiritual growth, and unless one belongs to a group that shares these assumptions, they are very alienating. In order for the statements to cease being generalizations, the life-changing experience linked with the statement needs to be shared. Without such personal sharing, the statements keep people strangers and prevent the building of a trusting community.

The second obstacle was the reality that many women's experiences did not fit into traditional male spiritual and religious categories. We have seen this most in women who are in the church but have lost their own sense of self and spirituality by identifying with a male deity or hierarchy to the exclusion of their own femaleness and its goodness. This is also evidenced by women who have left the church or have become very alienated from traditional church settings because their life experience is so acutely absent.

Women have had to undergo a variety of emotional and intellectual gyrations to fit their experience into male categories, such as becoming "sons" of God. The absence, denial, and trivialization of the feminine in Christian theology, liturgy, and practice has always been painful. The repression and denial that some women have undergone in order to fit their experience into a male mold has cost them dearly. Denying one's feminine self, either consciously or unconsciously, is enraging; getting in touch with the experience of this anger can be daunting. But it can also be a catalyst for great spiritual growth and regeneration.

The absence of the feminine in Western spirituality is becoming an increasingly urgent issue in the life of the church. How can a woman seek spiritual guidance from an institution that does not value the feminine? Many women have answered by leaving the church. Others have stayed, some have returned, and many are seeking a new expression of church that values women and the feminine. In the seeking, certain questions have arisen as to why the feminine has been so devalued. Through discussion, sharing of lives, historical research, and feminist theologizing, women have found that the roots of their oppression are bound up in the patriarchal philosophy of dualism.

Women and men today are the inheritors of dualistic thinking: the either/or system that places all persons, places, and ideas in sets of opposites such as right/wrong, good/bad, necessary/unnecessary. If one side is right, the other side is wrong. Therefore, if thinking is good/right/necessary, then the physical is wrong/bad/unnecessary. The classic sets of dualisms are male/light/good/spirit/eternal life and female/darkness/evil/matter/natural death.

In other words, to choose the feminine is to be on the wrong side. Many religious experts will maintain that male and female are equal, that God has no gender, and that the Bible uses many images for God, including God as Mother. But try saying, "Our Mother who art in heaven, hallowed be thy name . . ." How does it feel?

Most Western thinking has chosen to adhere to dualism and forego the creativity that is demanded to move beyond it. Dualistic thinking is easy; it is "systematic" and self-referential. You can figure out a right or wrong pattern and quickly arrive at a cohesive, if destructively simplistic, answer. The choice to maintain dualism has to do with *power over* and the ability to control. Dualism works to keep the deck permanently stacked against those without power in our society. It works neatly with racism, sexism, classism, heterosexism, and all the other -isms.

Because of dualism, women's sexuality has been linked with sin. In the church and society, anything female and sexual has been scrupulously excised, avoided, allegorized into acceptability, or used to enforce male domination of women. Guilt over a so-called original sin transmitted through human sexuality (which is to say, female sexuality) has worked very well to keep women in their "place" and out of the spheres of power and empowerment. By ritually, theologically, philosophically, and psychologically defaming female sexuality, women are kept alienated from themselves.

Since women's sexuality has been identified with sin, it is easy to see how dualism is a major obstacle in the development of a healthy spirituality. It is antithetical to reconciliation, the task to which Christians are called. Prophetic reconciliation truthfully names the disease. This is the first step in healing, and it cannot take place while maintaining a dualistic worldview.

Reconciliation of the body/mind and sexuality/spirituality dualisms has been central in living out a healthy spirituality during the training and for the trainers in their own lives. We discovered that we could not talk about feminine spirituality without addressing our sexuality.

We heard a variety of stories from women during the training sessions about how the dualisms of good/male/spiritual and bad/female/sexual had been manifested in their lives. One woman told of her marriage to a priest who would not have intercourse if the sacraments were in the

We don't discuss sex, and we NEVER do energizers.

house. Another woman told of how her husband, soon to be ordained a priest, would not assist at the birth of their child because he did not want to be defiled by the birth blood.

One woman priest told of her bishop, who forbade her to administer the sacraments when she was menstruating. Women who heard this story, many of whom opposed the ordination of women at the outset of the training, were transformed by their relationship with her as a priest and a woman. On the last night of their time together, they had a "consecration" of this woman as a bishop. It was made even more wonderful by the fact that she was menstruating! This group, through its relationship with this woman, spiritually healed the wound to her self-esteem and sexuality that had hampered her ability to accept herself as a priest and use all the power of her sexuality in her priesthood.

In another group, one woman insisted that menstrual taboos were biblical and had to be adhered to in regard to ordination. Another woman responded that there were similar taboos for men about ejaculation but that had not prevented men from being ordained or celebrating the eucharist. The trends in selective readings of Scripture underscore and uphold the spirituality/sexuality split and how it is used to disempower.

The lack of a tradition that values the feminine, coupled with slogans based on assumptions that block dialogue rather than facilitate mutual understanding were hurdles we encountered in every training event. Both stoppers keep women from defining their own experience, even when they are in a place that is specifically for that purpose. No wonder it was difficult for us to formulate a congruent experiential learning section on spirituality! How did we approach it finally? We focused on our lives and told stories about our experience of ourselves, the feminine, the holy.

In order to approach the difficult task of speaking about spirituality, we took as our starting point the question posed by Episcopal laywoman Verna Dozier in her life and work: *When do you feel most fully you?* This question is the beginning place for seeking congruity between who you are, what you feel, what your gifts are, and how these qualities are lived out in your life. Is there congruity between your feelings, gifts, vision, and your life as it is now? These are the questions we ask of ourselves and the participants in the training.

The training affirms an overall sense that each of us is a note sung by God in the opus that is creation. There will never be another like you.

Part of our task on earth is to find that note and sing it. Our God wants something from each of us and has equipped us in order that we might do exactly that which gives us the most joy and sense of completeness. Our life work is to find that note, deal with the obstacles that come between us and its fullest expression, and then find others whose song is sung with ours. Each trainer feels differently about spirituality, but we agree that we feel most fully ourselves—most centered, rooted, and fully alive—when we are engaged in our call or ministry. We know it because it feels natural; it is not a great strain to undertake it. We feel more of who we are and not less; we feel enriched and not impoverished when we give our gift away to the world. Aoteoroan (New Zealander) Kiri Te Kanawa sings opera because she is gifted with the "knowing" to sing it. No amount of training can give it to her; it can enhance the gift but cannot create it. Guatemalan author Rigoberta Menchu is a storyteller of the oppression of her people. She learned Spanish in order to speak to the world, but learning Spanish did not give her the gift of eloquence. The expression—the giving of our gifts to the world—is an event surrounded by great power. When we give our gifts, we are powerful. Some of us know our whole lives what we are given to do; others must go on a journey of discovery.

Sometimes we cannot hear our calls to ministry because of an "internal monitor" that teaches us to be our inhibitor. This internal monitor has been named the "internalized oppressor" by a variety of groups. The purpose of the internalized oppressor is to maintain a disvalued sense of the feminine for both women and men. The internalized monitor/oppressor helps to keep us separate from one another and suspicious of ourselves and each other. The internalized monitor/oppressor prevents community among women from happening. We watch ourselves; we watch each other. We keep ourselves excluded.

This type of separation keeps us distrustful of ourselves and one another. All of this feeds into a culture already staggering under the weight of individualism. Our lives are lived a-relationally without consideration for the collective community. This has led us to the brink of disaster. Feminist thought and action now realize that relationality is normative and that we only become ourselves as we exist in community with others. This small statement represents a quantum leap in both actual experience and philosophical thought.

The small word *relationality* provides the basis for the phrase I use to describe the leadership training: "self-making in community."

Relationality conditions our spirituality and continues to move in and through the rest of our lives.

Throughout the training and in the section on sexuality and spirituality, we invite the participants to share in small groups and explore their calls—their ministry—and to examine what has sped their journey and what has hindered it. When do they feel most fully alive now? In this process of dialogue and experience, women articulate their theology and share their spirituality. The process is, at its roots, relational. We discover ourselves in community.

In order to find ways in which we could incorporate, so to speak, our embodied selves in the training and move away from intellectualized sessions, we decided to include "energizers" throughout the day. These exercises are designed to get people in touch with their bodies. Each of us led one of the morning energizers, and we could do anything that we felt good about. I chose to teach some Middle Eastern women's folk dancing. This style of dancing is wonderfully centering and energizing. It helps our thinking selves to learn from our womanness, our bodies. Many women, however, feel ambivalent about this type of dance. Once women did this dancing for fun and to encourage one another in childbirth. But later it was stolen, trivialized, made pornographic, and reduced to "belly dancing."

I introduced the energizer with my version of the creation of Israel. I noted the great irony that the first liturgical act of Israel to celebrate God's giving birth to them down the channel and through the salt waters of the Red Sea was probably "belly dancing." Just as they would have done at the birth of a new child, Miriam and her sisters took up their timbrels and danced for the birth of a new people, praising its mother, Yahweh, for triumphing in safely bringing her child to birth.

Because of this, I have stopped using the term *belly dancing* and instead use *birth dancing.*

The team had decided that I would do my energizer on the day we presented the sexuality/spirituality section. Those women who wished to participate in the energizer yawned their way into the meeting room, ready for some kind of aerobic "jazz-you-up-for-the-day" movement. When I announced what the energizer would be, there were a few squeals and cries of "Oh no!" We joked about what else they were not going to be able to tell their husbands about this training. Some women asked, "Do we have to do it for our husbands when we go home?" This told me just how deeply their sexuality had been alienated from their sense of themselves. Even here in the company of women, some thought first of their husband's ownership of their bodies and their sexuality. Others felt ashamed of their bodies and looked to see if others were heavier or slimmer than they were.

I gathered the women into a circle and led them through some stretches and then into weight shifting. There we were: a large circle of women shifting our weight from foot to foot, moving through the mid-point where the weight is evenly distributed between the feet, our legs open and power moving up from the earth and through our bodies. Then we increased the speed and added a delayed flip of the hip, building speed and tension while feeling the increasing energy circling our wombs, circling the room. The nervous giggles and uncertainty were slowly changing into intense concentration as I led the group into an increasingly intricate pattern. There is a fierce and wonderful joy in groups of women dancing for themselves, dancing for their own delight, dancing away from being self-conscious to self-awareness. Too soon the time was over, and others began drifting in the room. In self-defense, some of the dancers began to make jokes about their "belly dancing," but I could sense the pleasure emanating from some—pleasure and pride in their women's bodies.

Being assertive with our spirits, our minds, and our bodies—this is a powerful combination. It is no wonder that women have been consistently led away from valuing their powerful bodies, from having ownership of them. The morning's energizer opened the way for "Aha's" as the day progressed and served as a catalyst for the evening's work on sexuality and spirituality.

As we moved through the sections "Understanding Power" and "Valuing Our Differences," there was some intense energy around the women's perceptions of their sexuality. In the "Understanding Power" section, one woman, a law enforcement officer, shared how she had had to file suit against her sergeant in order to have pornographic photographs removed from the station. An extremely powerful woman, she knew that her presence was threatening to some of her male coworkers. She felt that the photographs were explicit attempts to reduce her power as an officer. "It's as if they think that by having those pictures there they can say to me that, no matter what I do, I'm still just an object to be taken and used and thrown away just like the magazines—powerless and vulnerable just like the women in those magazines."

Even though the suit had cost her the support of her colleagues, she felt that she had gained in her own sense of personal power and in *defining her own sexuality.* Her sense of ownership and self-determination took her sexuality out of the male/subject/manipulator and female/object/manipulated power configuration that distorts most male/female relationships. Sexism had served to distort her sense of her own sexuality by using it as an unwholesome power leverage to force her into so-called acceptable female sexual behavior.

During the training, she got in touch with feelings of being suppressed in her work. In police work, she was being called upon to "be a man"; her feminine self was a disability and not an asset. In going along with this notion, she felt she had lost an important piece of herself, a piece that had initially led her into police work. She realized that part of her spiritual work would be to discover how she could be most fully herself—including her sexuality—and function within her job. She decided not to quit her job or suppress her feelings but to find new ways beyond the subject/object type of male/female relationships and sexual expression. All of us affirmed her in this wonderful realization and in her resolve to stay on the job and work on the situation.

Both gender and sexuality are distorted by sexism, which forces us away from positive valuations of our gender and our sexuality. In redefining our relationship to power and coercive *power over,* our sexuality begins to emerge as a positive empowering force in our lives. Claiming our sexuality helps us to be who we are instead of tailoring our actions to meet the standards of others. A substantive part of the empowerment comes simply from being with other women who value their sexuality and honestly confront the exterior forces and interior monitors that devalue their sexuality. Hearing others affirm their womanness is empowering because it is a new voice, one that affirms and does not negate our sexuality as "shameful" or "dirty" or powerless.

Negative sexual messages are a powerful package of lies to untie. Women untie these lies by stepping out of disempowering sexist stereotypes such as "sex kitten," "matron," "dried up old woman," "spinster," "mannishness," which reduce us to objects. Realizing that our sexuality is positive and powerful expands our options of behavior out of the stereotypes and into an expression of ourselves. We are sexual instead of "acting sexy." Sexuality becomes part of our power to create instead of manipulate.

One participant came to a leadership training event feeling down, old, and unattractive—she was buying into the stereotypes. During the course of the training, she shared her feelings. Her struggle opened the way for others to talk for the first time about their sexual self-perception. At the end of the training she felt revivified, "re-juiced," and rejuvenated through our "Yes!" to herself as a sexual and alive person.

A positive valuation of our sexuality is key to a healthy and creative expression of power and powerful leadership. When we are at home in our bodies, we know where we stand—in ourselves—and others know where and how they can stand in relationship to us. We don't "pull punches" by introducing inappropriate and split-off sexual behavior. We can recognize split-off sexual behavior because it is incongruent with the rest of our behavior. It "comes out of nowhere," a "loose cannon" that introduces an element of danger or distrust that can grow and eventually destroy a relationship, a project, a community. Inappropriate sexuality can also be used to get what one wants.

"Queen bee" types are notorious for inappropriate use of their sexuality to gain and use power. Rape, incest, child molestation, and sexual harassment constitute power abuse. Issues of inappropriate sexual behavior are almost always linked to abuse of power and feelings of powerlessness. Abuse of sexual power is the desire for power in and of itself—not for the use of the community. Inappropriate sexual behavior is about seeking *power over* another; it is not about love or mutuality. Because sexuality is powerful, we want it to be part of our conscious selves. There is no room in responsible leadership for sexuality that is lived out inappropriately by men or women.

That evening, we began to explore our feelings about what spirituality means in each of our lives. The work during the day on power; the -isms of racism and sexism; the valuing of differences; and the ongoing exploration of what womanness was for each of us—these had created a wonderful, yeasty mix into which we were now adding spirituality. This spirituality was in relation to our sexuality.

That night I shared a story about a turning point in my ministry. At the time of this story, I was trying to discern for myself whether or not I had a call to the priesthood. As part of this discernment process, I had become a lay reader. I was also working at the Women in Mission and Ministry (WIMM) office at the Episcopal Church Center and was in the painful process of raising my consciousness. Even as I was responding to a call to the priesthood, I was becoming aware of just what kind of institution housed this priesthood and the antics that went on inside it. I seriously doubted I could be a priest and maintain my integrity. Part of my work at the WIMM office had been to assemble the "official" documents surrounding the women's ordination struggle in the sixties and seventies. I was shocked when I encountered some of the reasons that women's ordination was opposed. Everything had been invoked from Bronze-age cultic prohibitions about menstruation to women being transmitters of Original Sin, to the Deutero-Pauline injunctions against women speaking in church. I was even more shocked when, using those same injunctions, certain brothers and sisters in my parish began to question my call—even though the Episcopal Church had approved the ordination of women several years earlier. I was getting a full-blown experience of institutional sexism in the church—how widespread it is and how much work there is to do to overcome it. I was becoming discouraged.

During Lent that year, my parish hosted a Wednesday supper with speakers who also preached at the evening service. It was my turn to read and serve at the altar. I had not really looked at the speaker schedule. That night, to my horror, our guest was one of the most vociferous opponents of women's ordination. Just reading his words, long ago spoken, had hurt. I suddenly felt awkward in a place where I had felt so at home. I felt foreign in the sanctuary that I so deeply loved. And then I remembered I was menstruating. Before I had entered the church as an adult, I had no more than the "usual" discomfort about my bodily functions. Like most women, I hoped the person at the drugstore counter was a woman when I bought tampons. But I never thought of menstruation as a violating thing, an unclean thing, an unholy thing. It was just part of me. Only when I started reading about these things in theological and ecclesiastical discussions did I grow uncomfortable. Against my better judgment, against what I knew and valued about myself, I found myself blushing with shame as I approached the altar. As I climbed the chancel steps and looked up I saw the displeasure on this "great" man's face. I was furious with my curate, who knew this person well and had not been sensitive to the implications of our presence together at the altar. I felt "set up."

Being the church's special guest for the evening, this man celebrated the eucharist. As we approached the rail to administer communion, I trailed behind with the chalice. For the first time I felt that my call as a eucharistic minister was wrong. The visiting priest began slapping wafers into the hands of the communicants, my sisters and brothers in

Christ. I gave the chalice, as usual. Suddenly I was aware that this priest was standing behind me, fairly tapping his foot with impatience. He had finished with the bread on the first round and was coming full steam up behind me. I felt flustered and forgot the call, "The Blood of Christ, the Cup of Salvation." I knew that this man heard the mumbling and stumbling I was making. "He's chalking up another reason why women should not be allowed to administer the sacraments," I thought. My curate came up behind me and said, "Hurry up!" I wanted to cry. I wanted to leave.

I had totally bought into the voice inside that constantly reminds us of what Ann Wilson Schaef calls the "original sin of being born female." The inescapable "sin" is the knowledge that we are only women, that we were born "wrong," and because we were born "wrong," there is nothing we can do to be right. I had given up my power. I gave this stranger, who didn't know me from Eve, the power to define who I was based on his debased perceptions of women. I was doing the oppressor's job for him!

At the same time that I realized this, I saw the face of my beloved sister Claudia looking up into my face, waiting for the words to which we would both say amen. That amen seemed to echo around me. I felt a wonderful rush of power as I looked, and there was my brother John waiting, too, for the words that bound us together, sister to brother, equal to equal. I felt the dance then, the spiral of energy that passes through the cup and between the family. It knits us together. Our collected, energized spirits unite in the wine, sealed in the blood of communion/community.

In that moment, the chains of the internal voices fell off and lost their power. The huffing of the man, for he was only one man and not God or the Church, ceased to oppress me. I came home again to the eucharist. Through God's working in my community, I was brought to mindfulness, or repentance, of the sin of trying to make myself less than what God had made me. I was giving up the power that was my responsibility to bear into the world. I was ready to listen to any external voice, abandon my own knowledge and perceptions, and abandon God's desire for my life. Yet when I listened to my deepest self, the self wherein God lives and moves and has Being with me, I was blessed and made whole in my community. In my sister's and brother's amen, I heard the yes of God—the yes that affirms the power within and disarms false *power over.* No one can take your power unless you give it to them.

The spiritual journey requires struggle and sacrifice. In my experience of communion that day, I experienced both: struggle to come through to consciousness about the reality of my situation and sacrifice in that I gave up my dependency and my learned powerlessness. A new world started for me on that day. I now had to be responsible for the stewardship of the gifts I had been given. The experience was liberating, the hallmark of God's presence.

Relationships, self-definition, community, sexuality, spirituality, divinity—dare we look into ourselves for the answers? Dare we claim that we are the house and the household of God and that we hold the answers to our questions? Yes, we can and must. We learn to trust and love ourselves as the home of God and not the source of Original Sin. Our sexuality is not an obstacle but a door to God. In this loving and trusting, we will come to know what is authentically feminine, what is authentically masculine, and what is authentically divine. All are bound up together in a wonderful cosmic birthing dance. Sexuality is in spirituality; the feminine is in the divine. Linda Hurcombe, editor of *Sex and God*, writes the following:

> Sexuality is a . . . diffuse and symbolic term. It both includes and transcends biological organ states. It is a basic dimension of our personhood. It permeates and affects all our feelings, thoughts and actions. It is our self-understanding and way of being in the world as female. Sexuality involves much more than what we do with our genitals. It is who we are as body selves who experience the emotional, cognitive, physical and spiritual need for intimate communion, human and divine. It is clear that an understanding of women's sexuality is essential to a full understanding of what it means to be made in God's image.

Women are imagers of God through our lives of loving, reaching out, nurturing, protecting, struggling, birthing, being for ourselves, and being with others. In the fierce, glad joy of womanliness, we reveal who God is to each other, to our brothers, to the world. Without the knowing that only women can bring by their imaging of God, human understanding and knowing of God is incomplete and false. We are reduced to worshiping idols. Without the depth that both male and female bring to our understanding of God, we end up with a stereotypic god, one that carries the image of power as it is currently defined and helps implement and uphold that power. Stereotypical images of God are easy to manipulate and use destructively. Stereotypical gods keep us from letting be what is.

To carry and be God's image is to take up responsibility. It is, as the Chinese say, to hold up half the sky. When women accept themselves as holy beings, their spirituality as good and true, their sexuality as whole and wholesome, this contributes to a more real understanding of ourselves and of God.

The embodied, sexual reality of women has brought healing in many of the training sessions and brought home the reality of woman as *imago dei*, Christ bearer, women incarnating deity together in community. The spirituality that has emerged transforms the community: through telling stories; through analyzing power and revealing where women have been empowered and disempowered; and through experiencing the painful absence of the feminine in our lives, our culture, our religion.

Feeling this absence reveals the longing for wholeness and the reaching out to others, to women who affirm one another and hear each other's stories. This experience feeds our passion for the wholeness to which God calls us, our desire to grow and become the healing arms of our God. This God, present in the moment, says with every woman's birth into selfhood, "This is my daughter with whom I am well pleased." This is self-making in community.

Questions for Reflection:
1. When do you feel most fully you? When do you feel most fully alive?
2. What positive internal messages do you have about your sexuality? What are the negative messages? What messages affect your experience of God?
3. Are you able to experience or envision the feminine in the deity? If yes, how? If not, why?
4. Considering the broad spectrum of bodiliness that feminine sexuality encompasses, where and how have you encountered the feminine in the divine? How has this affected your own sense of self?

FREEDOM TO BE ME

Edna M. Brown

My story as a leadership trainer is a metaphor for my life, at least so far. It seems that so many of my richest experiences have come about as I am making other plans. It is not that I feel powerless in my life. Rather, I at last have accepted the great gift that I have been given.

After graduating from the University of Chicago in March 1960 with a bachelor's degree in political science that was more like liberal arts, I relocated to California. For me, a true child of the 1960s, the only possible action was to find myself in the land of sunshine. My first job was a federal appointment with the Air Force in San Bernardino, California. The most memorable thing about this experience was that it reinforced the happy relationship I have continued to have with the wonderful world of serendipity. In San Bernardino I met my husband, Don. After a brief courtship, we married in July 1960. Shortly afterward, we moved to Oakland, California, and I began my long and fruitful career in the nonprofit sector. This involved work with training programs that received federal, state, and foundation funding. My training history goes back to these early days when I and others believed that we could change the world or at least make a difference. As a high-energy person, I was simultaneously bringing up a stepdaughter and three children born to us. Earning a master's degree at the University of California at Berkeley somehow fit into my plans for 1970. It was years before I discovered that other people did these things one at a time.

My involvement with the Women's Leadership Training Program is a rather convoluted story. It began in Michigan, where we had moved after leaving California. I was interested in bringing my consulting business to Michigan while still maintaining my national work. One day, I mentioned to my sister, an Episcopal priest, that I would be interested in doing more training with women in the church. She said that she knew Ann Smith at the Episcopal Church Center and would ask her about the training program. As it happened, my sister had reason to call Ann that week, and she mentioned that she knew a trainer if Ann was interested. She did not tell Ann that I was her sister so that Ann would not be put in the awkward position of being pressured by friendship.

That very week, a trainer had to drop out of a training event scheduled for the Upper Peninsula of Michigan. Ann called me about a week prior to the workshop and asked if I would be interested. As Ann described the work to me, I became very excited. I believe in the empowerment of women, and the idea of work that was so rewarding and also spiritually based seemed perfect. I had very high expectations for the experience and was especially interested in meeting the team of trainers. Although this all happened a very short time ago, I now feel that I have become lasting friends as well as colleagues with these other trainers. The team was made up of Ann Smith, Sandy Stewart, Linda Grenz, and me. We are very different women and modeled the possibilities that the training addressed: there is no "right way" to be a woman today, and we all have choices, some that we make and some that we passively accept.

Between the discussion with Ann and the start of the training, I received my training manual. It was so filled with rich material and ideas that I wondered if we could share it effectively with the participants. (I still feel that the manual is a gold mine and hope that participants will use it as a life-long resource.)

No one called me about where or how we would meet at the Marquette, Michigan, airport. After calling my conference contact, I determined that we would need a site to meet before the conference and go over other details. Later I learned that it is typical to have a trainer designated to handle these details. It just seemed disorganized to me, especially as a new person on the team. However, I am nothing if not a lemonade-maker out of lemons, and I set about filling this particular gap.

The great day of the trip to the Upper Peninsula arrived. So did I, but between my departure from Traverse City and my arrival at Marquette, my luggage missed a connection. This was not too horrible, but my precious and well-thumbed manual was in my suitcase. I did the mature thing—I yelled and carried on. Needless to say, it was to no avail. My luggage arrived later that night as it would have if I had remained calm. Another lesson learned and the training had not even begun.

This brings to mind another of my behaviors. I must be ever-vigilant to my great tendency to "mom" and "help" others. For me that begins with monitoring my mouth. One of my weaknesses is a need to include everyone in everything. That often takes the form of talk that says "we all" or "everyone is" and similar "we" statements. One principle we agreed on early was to model speaking for self and challenging each other when this is violated. I hear a lot of "And what does Edna think?" But it helps, and I take notice. I find "I" statements so much cleaner and clearer that I very rarely want to gain power by speaking for others.

One of the hallmarks that makes up my "Edna-ness" is a strong sense of humor and a very sunny spirit. I know, however, what a very successful distancing technique humor can be, and I used it a lot with this new group. This seems to be a coping method so natural that it may be part of my very being. As a black woman, I am never sure what is adaptive to dealing with race in a "white" world or what is personal style or synergy.

Sometimes, I am amazed that this is a consulting job, since I learn and gain so many insights about myself. When I review this leadership training experience, I find my most successful learning has taken place in my efforts to be authentic with the staff and participants. There are some "Aha!" moments for me when bits of the training experience seem especially real. I have organized these experiences as they occurred over the five-day training period.

Day 1

My first time as a trainer was also my first experience with the program, which meant that I had never before experienced the exercises. The first activity was an icebreaker to help participants become acquainted with each other and the staff. A training team member led a discussion about the power of names and naming, and shared something about her own name. After the short introduction, the participants and training team members were given markers, pens, colored paper, ribbons, tape, scissors, and staplers. Each woman was to express her name or something about her name with the materials. This naming icebreaker was not natural for me. I am not artsy-craftsy, and I have no hidden need or interest to express myself this way. The narrative material, on the other hand, was a revelation to me. I loved the emotional response to the meaning of one's name. This could have gone on forever, and I still feel lots of energy around this activity. As I observed the making of name tags and realized their usefulness as a talking tool, I freed myself to participate. But best of all, I granted Edna the permission to do enough of this to get by with a little help from her friends—without feeling that she must *love* the exercise. Over time, there has been a metamorphosis in this exercise for me. Initially, I revealed little of myself, just a bit of my feelings about being named for an aunt. Today I can relate more of my feelings and provide more thoughtful information.

Day 2: Empowerment

So many women are skittish about the word *power*. It is very hard to move from the hierarchical "more for me, less for you" model of power to the love concept of infinite power that grows as it is used and extended to others. The session on empowerment has become richer for me as it has moved from a lecture format to an experiential sharing piece with participants actively using the material to have an impact on their work.

One memorable time, I trained with Linda while Sandy and Kathy Tyler Scott scored Myers-Briggs instruments. At one point, I gave participants fifteen minutes for an exercise and looked back to see Linda reminding me that I was about thirty minutes over my time. Talk about whoops! Luckily the team could do what the participants were encouraged to do: stop and review what had happened and identify learnings. This was a very effective way out. As a result, the material was redesigned to become the experiential component it should have been.

Day 3: Critical Skills

Assertiveness and anger were areas that required lots of growth and self-awareness for me. I live easily at the intellectual level and am very good at "knowing" the psychologically correct postures, but I have sensitive points around these areas. Conflict is difficult for me. When people raise voices and disagree, I get uneasy. I prefer peace at any price. But of course, the price can be too high, especially if it costs one's self-respect and personal integrity. As I have participated in the training programs, I have learned to respect my own style—warts and all—yet I have become much more comfortable with honest differences of opinion.

Day 4: Brokenness

Understanding biases, prejudices, and -isms is very powerful. It produces some real questions for me as an African-American trainer. Most of the groups have been all white, and the few others had limited numbers of women of color. This sometimes made me feel that my presence on the staff represented premature engagement with a woman of color. I still remember a session when I mentioned how frequently white people say to me that they never think of me as African-American but as a person. How odd that these same people would describe someone as having colored her hair with Clairol number 2 or as wearing a plaid skirt. I usually shared that no one ever describes her garden as having flowers. ("I don't know what kinds, I just see flowers.") Some people could relate to this, but some could not move past their defenses. I feel that the whole task is less and less appropriate for a black trainer and better undertaken in a same-race encounter. This is reinforced as I review the training experiences with another black trainer, Kathy Tyler Scott. In Stony Point, New York, Kathy was the trainer assigned to coordinate with the staff person at the conference site, and that staff person found every excuse to ask questions of each of the two white trainers. She "forgot" that Kathy was the coordinator. Conveniently, she seemed to always remember that I was not the assigned liaison and so never asked me questions. These types of experience occurred at several levels—with the staff, with participants informally, and even with the Myers-Briggs integration exercises (no pun intended). In the morning, we discussed how our brokenness affects our perceptions, choices, and behaviors.

Where is mine?

Day 5: A New Path

It always seems a long way from start to finish for me. Every time I have learned a lot—mostly about me. I never go home again the same person, but I am the sum of all the experiences I have ever had, including leadership training.

Questions for Reflection:

1. Some people plan their work and then work their plan. Chance plays no role in their work life. What about in your life?

2. When you experience difference in small areas, such as in ordering a meal or choosing a dress, do you compare, believing that difference implies a best/worse choice? How about in larger areas? To you, does difference mean alternative or does it mean inferior/superior?

3. If using "we" talk rather than "I" statements feels better to you, what do you gain? What do you lose?

4. How can you begin to share your true feelings about race, color, and class differences with those of your same race, color, and class? Why should you?

POWER: THE PERILS OF PYRAMIDS

Ann Smith

Power in the hierarchical organizations of churches and most businesses is based on an unequal model of power. Power is defined as *power over* others in which a few make the decisions for the majority. People are treated according to their position in the structure: those who are closest to the top of the pyramid have the most power. They have the greatest amount of access to information, money, and the resources needed to carry out the work. Those on the bottom of the pyramid have the least amount of power. All decisions are made for them by those above, and they must carry out the work with the resources given them.

In this system, power is experienced as finite; that is, a limited amount of resources, money, and information can be shared, depending on the individual's position in the pyramid. It is understood that, as more power is given away to others, the less there is for those on top. Power is experienced as scarce; to share or give away power is to lose power. This understanding of power is destructive to individuals, races, nations, the earth, and ultimately all God's creation. Significantly, this system of management no longer is accepted as an efficient model for business or for the institutional churches. Rosabeth Moss Kanter of the Harvard Business School has reversed the conventional statement on power, saying, "Powerlessness corrupts. Absolute powerlessness corrupts absolutely."

Empowerment or *power within and throughout* is the new model that is rapidly changing business structures from a rigid pyramid to a structure with fewer organizational layers. The churches are remembering the more egalitarian model of the early church. If a business is to remain profitable, it can no longer become another pyramid. Likewise, the churches can no longer thrive as viable institutions into the twenty-first century if they do not develop nonhierarchical models of power. They must do so if they are to empower the laity, who comprise the vast majority of the church. We can begin to experience the kingdom when all creation is equally valued and equally shares the abundance of God's riches.

There will be a power struggle at some point.

As individuals in our own organizations, we can choose a form of empowerment that will enable individuals to equally share the power. Power becomes empowerment when each one of us experiences God's empowerment and when we, in turn, help others by sharing information and resources to live out the fullness of who we are and who we can become. Sharing our stories and listening to others are the most powerful forms of resource sharing that I have experienced, for everyone has life experiences they can share. In a nonhierarchical, circular model, leadership is shared and each individual is seen as having something to contribute. Power is experienced as an abundance of information and resources for all. The belief in the adage "the more I give away, the more I have" becomes a reality—even for those in top leadership positions. By sharing leadership and enabling others to do the same, we diminish our fear of relinquishing power.

One example of empowerment expressed in the training program is the enormous amount of love we felt when we bonded with our first child. In loving my first child, I did not have less love to give to my husband, nor when the second child was born did I have less love for the first child. Instead, I had more love to give and giving it freely was very natural. In the group, we talked about how the more we gave to others, the more we had to give. We need to equate empowerment with love, the greatest gift of all. "God so loved the world that God gave his only begotten son that whosoever believes in him will have everlasting life."

Another example given in the training program is the presentation of apple seeds. Kathy Tyler Scott distributes apple seeds to each participant, demonstrating that there are plenty of seeds to go around. We discuss how each one of us has the potential to grow our own apple tree from a tiny seed and produce more than we received. We talk about how we can move away from the thinking of scarcity toward the realities of abundance. When we empower others, we receive more in return.

I also draw a pyramid on newsprint to demonstrate the hierarchical model of power, placing the different staff positions and departments of the national church where they are located in the structure. Our unit, Women in Mission and Ministry, is given a circle with adjoining circles marking the women's groups with which we relate. Each training event is also given a circle. As the number of circles increases, we can clearly see from the drawing a change of power that is having an impact on the pyramid. This graphic demonstration, in which the participants of each training event can visualize their part in the church structure and can begin to change the church (through changing their own power models), creates a sense of excitement. I feel a tingling sensation in my body as the energy from the women in the room increases, each person adding to the group's synergy.

How can you begin to influence others to change the models of power from a hierarchical to a circular model? A favorite fable from my childhood is the story of the wind challenging the sun to a contest to determine the more powerful. Whoever could remove the coat from the man walking down the road would be the more powerful, the wind decreed. The wind blew harder and harder to blow off the man's coat, but the more he blew, the tighter the man held on to his coat. In contrast, the sun shone down upon the man, warming him until the man was comfortable enough to take off his coat.

The early church grew from attraction. More and more people wanted what Christianity had to offer, and it became a worldwide religion. I believe that more and more people are ready for a new model of power. The changes needed to transform pyramids into circles will happen in the same way the sun easily enabled the man to remove his coat. Just as the man felt it was natural to remove his coat, so the circular system will come about as more people feel right about a new model of power.

In an equal power model, the means and not the end is justified. What matters is how we treat one another, how we interrelate and interact with all of God's creation. Martin Luther King taught us that all life is interrelated, all humanity part of one process, and to the degree that I harm another, I am harming myself.

When I model a different way of interacting with others, I effect change. When groups effect change within a system, the entire organization is changed. When a "critical mass" of the population effects change, a movement is started and systems are transformed. Just as a worldwide liberation movement is bringing down walls between nations and toppling hierarchical governments, we, too, can effect change and will do so by changing ourselves, our families, and the organizations in which we are involved.

An influential book for me and many other women in the eighties was *Games My Mother Never Taught Me*. It is a practical guide that teaches women to play the power game as well as men. It is *not* a book that attempts to change the system. It is about how to succeed like a man in the organization. Women have had major successes in breaking down barriers to nontraditional jobs. We consequently have become successful in many hierarchies by being assimilated into the structure, receiving recognition and rewards by becoming "junior men." The cost to us as women has been that the systems did not change and the feminine—that quality needed to restore balance to the masculine power structures—has suffered in maintaining a system incompatible to our nature.

I believe that important books for the nineties will be based on "games my mother taught me." In playing mother to my dolls, kittens, and puppies, I learned how to nurture others and how to be in harmonious relationships to people and animals. Jumping rope taught me when to come in and when to go out and how to be in relationship to my teammates' rhythm. Jumping rope is not so much about who wins but about who can move in rhythm with others. The goal is to be in relationship to ourselves and to others. We must teach others to be aware of differences and to be in relationship to different rhythms. Carol Gilligan's *A Different Voice* documents that women think and reason differently than men. Her work is backed by extensive research performed at Harvard University that is aiding women to value who we are and helping men to value our differences. We think in relationship to people, places, and things. Our reasoning is circular in pattern rather than linear.

The games "King of the Mountain" and "Master of the Universe" can no longer continue in our world. The devastating effects of *power over* must be reversed by substituting a new order of being in relationship to people and to all of God's creation. We can no longer enable the destructive power games in our families, in our groups, and in our organizations. These games are destroying the environment and threatening the multiplicity of races and cultures. As women, we must learn to reject a position of powerlessness. We can no longer tolerate corruption of ourselves or of our institutions. We must value the feminine and bring about a process of integration instead of assimilation in which the feminine/masculine is balanced in all facets of our lives. Through the circular model of power, we grow in strength and courage to bring changes to others. In community, the God in me meets the God in you.

At the end of the discussion on power, we hand out "power shirts"— white T-shirts with a sparkling red outline of a celtic cross and the words "Empowering Ourselves, Empowering Others" written inside the shape of the cross. With laughter and glee, we leave the training room and go to our power lunch where we talk about how women can make a difference.

Questions for Reflection:
1. How do you empower yourself?
2. What kind of power model do you have in your own family? Is it a hierarchical model in which the father has the most power and the youngest child the least?
3. Is your family based on the circular model in which every individual shares in the decisions and the individual who is the most invested in a particular decision has the most responsibility?
4. What groups are you a part of that use the circular model? (If you are in a Twelve Step program, you are part of a circular model.)
5. What is the structure and what is your position in the organizations where you are a volunteer or a paid employee?
6. Remembering that you cannot change others but by changing your own behavior you bring change to the structure, what can you do to bring about change in your organization? How are decisions made: by a few people for others or by consensus? Is the work style collaborative?

USING THE A-WORD

Katherine Tyler Scott

Smile. Be pleasant. Be nice. Be feminine. Act like a lady. None of these messages are bad. In fact, most are congruent with being a good person. As Christians, we want to exemplify and express love and respect for others. So what is the problem with these words? One major difficulty is that they have been used to reinforce our ambivalence about assertive behavior. If I am assertive, will I still be loved? Will I still be feminine? Will I still be a good person? Our answer to such fear-ridden questions is yes. We spend considerable time in leadership training helping participants understand what assertive behavior is and why it is important for them to develop it.

The social conditioning of females (and males) is so sex-role stereotyped that it is hard for any of us to be whole people. Assertiveness and its characteristics are those we have most often attributed to males. Males are affirmed for being direct, honest, clear, and able to disagree openly. Most females have not been affirmed for such behavior; indeed, many have been negatively labeled or put down, confirming their worst fears about the risks of being assertive. Assertiveness is a question of self-identity and self-regard: you know who you are and value yourself. Assertive people like and respect themselves, *and* they like and respect others. They are able to express themselves, their thoughts, and feelings in an open, honest, direct manner that is respectful of themselves and others. Such behavior optimizes the chance for resolution of conflict and the improvement of relationships, just as it increases confidence and self-esteem. While assertive behavior is no guarantor of getting what you want, it will increase your sense of personal power. It is important for women to know that assertive behavior is empowering—to self and to others.

Many women confuse assertiveness with aggressiveness. Aggressive behavior is the expression of one's thoughts and feelings at the expense of others; it is an exercise of *power over* others. I count; you do not. I'm up; you are down. It is attacking, belittling, hostile, and disrespectful so that others feel put down and alienated. Assertive and aggressive behavior is persistently confused because most women have been

DAY 1—STILL HIDING

_____

_____

_____

_____

_____

_____

socialized to be passive, and the move from passive behavior to assertive *feels* like a move to aggression. In fact, when changing from passive to assertive behavior, many people leap to being aggressive. Why? Our experience shows us that chronic passive behavior creates low self-esteem. It denies a person's right to an opinion or that person's rights in general. People who are taught to be passive are stuffers: they stuff their anger, any evidence of conflict, and their hurt. They are often silent sufferers—martyrs of emotions—and can be righteous about their "goodness." They are often perfect victims for aggressive people. All of this makes them prime candidates for blowing up!

Because of the social messages women have received about being assertive and because passivity is so devastating to a woman's spirit, many have learned to be passive-aggressive. Society has sanctioned such behavior for ages: the saying, "She's the power behind the throne," typifies this. It is OK to exercise power (i.e., to be assertive) as long as you do not demonstrate it publicly. What a bind! The very attempt to deny power leads to passive-aggressive behavior. We all know women whose personalities, skills, and experiences qualify them to lead any group or organization. They run their homes, families, communities, and churches, yet in the presence of men, they become door mice. Their voices are lost. Passive-aggressive behavior is a result of trying to deal with this double bind. It is a way to manipulate others to do what you want and remain powerful—but not in public. It involves indirect communication, splitting and "triangling"—the setting up of a third person to express your negative feelings about somebody else. Instead of speaking directly to the person you disagree with, you talk to everyone else but this person. As a result, others get angry for you. The costs of this behavior are similar to the costs of aggressive behavior. The major difference is that passive-aggressive behavior has an aura of politeness. As a friend of mine once said after an encounter with this behavior, "The knife goes in and out so nicely you don't realize you're bleeding until later." In leadership training sessions we focus on helping women see how destructive this behavior is.

Unfortunately, passive-aggressive behavior is often prevalent in women's groups. As a result, women have come to say very disparaging remarks about themselves. For example, "I don't trust women"; "I hate working with women"; "Women are sneaky and can't be trusted"; "That's just like women—bickering all the time"; and "Women aren't good leaders." Such comments reflect our internalized self-hatred and serve to perpetuate—not eliminate—this behavior.

We must remind ourselves that the roots of such behavior are founded in sanctions against power and assertiveness for women. Recognizing this helps us to understand and empathize, but it does not condone this kind of destructive behavior.

More than anything else, passive-aggressive behavior breeds distrust, which is deadly to any group and organization. This is aggression with a veneer of politeness, evil disguised in "Christian" behavior. That is what makes it so deadly. And this is why we stress the need to develop assertive behavior with women who are or will become leaders. The change begins with us—the leaders in the Church. Through awareness, modeling, mentoring, and practicing our skills, we can change our behavior and thus transform ourselves, our organizations, and our communities.

Leadership training explains these differences between assertive, aggressive, passive, and passive-aggressive behavior and participants are given examples of each. We then have an exercise in which the women reflect upon the messages they received early in their lives, messages that affect their behavior today. This is a very enlightening and cathartic time. Next we look at more positive messages we want for ourselves, and the women practice being more assertive in a special training session. This is only the *beginning* of months and years of practice. The trainers continue to practice, and we share what has worked for us.

We all must be intentional and conscientious about our behavior: We can *choose* to be doormats, dictators, manipulators, or assertive mentors and enablers. If we choose to be leaders, then we are responsible for acting in ways that increase the esteem and functioning of others. Assertiveness is a key element of effective leadership and a cornerstone for enabling change in the church and the world.

Questions for Reflection
1. Think of a time when you felt you were not assertive. What happened? How did you feel? What did you say or do? What was the result?
2. Think of a time when you felt you were assertive. What happened? How did you feel? What did you say or do? What was the result?
3. What helps you to be assertive?
4. What hinders you from being assertive?
5. How can you maintain your assertive behavior?

RENAMING, RECLAIMING

Alexsandra K. Stewart

I arrived at the training event feeling very much like the "new kid on the block" with all the nervousness that brings. In addition, a significant, long-term relationship had ended abruptly some months previously, and the lingering pain left me feeling especially vulnerable. I had been "Dear Jilled" while I was on a South Pacific island some ten thousand miles away from home and my support system. On my return, I had discovered that my financial assets had been plundered by the same person, someone I had trusted. At the time, I knew I was in pain. I now realize just how much those events changed me; in order to survive and complete my island contract, I had put myself into denial—at least that's how I perceived it at the time.

When I joined the training team, I was still denying the extent of the blow to my self-esteem and ashamed that I was still bothered by something that had happened over eight months ago. I could talk about it and laugh at myself for having been taken in by an expert con artist, but I felt a self-contempt for not having known better. Even though I shared some pieces of my story, I was guarded and hesitant to let people get very close to me. All the while, tears were very close to the surface. And although I was as open as I could be at the time, I know that I am more open today.

I imagine that my feelings were like those of many participants. They arrive at the training event eager for the experience, open to a point, yet a little fearful and not sure if it is safe to trust. They are unaware of how closed they are, of how fragile their self-esteem may be, or how deep their anger may run. Women come to the first evening of a leadership event wondering if they will be accepted as they are, with their own particular set of skills and imperfections. They may have an area about which they feel self contempt. They may be blaming themselves for an ended relationship or a sick parent. So they, too, are guarded or less open than they will be in the future.

I came with uncertainty to the first team meeting and planning session for Kentucky Leadership '85. I think it's a small leap of faith for the training team and for the participants to leave home and come. Just as

99

the first evening of a training event is planned for community building, the first meeting of the trainers is spent "getting on board" with each other: finding out what is important in each person's life, how they are doing, and what personal issues might affect the upcoming training.

I remember feeling a little "out of it" as we began to clarify our work together. There was the past history and previous experiences that Pat Moore, Kathy Tyler Scott, and Ann Smith had shared. There was a short-hand communication happening at times, and I grew tired of asking for explanations. I felt competent to do the material yet still wondered if I were being judged. There seemed to be some tension.

Given my recent experiences, I was not trusting my perceptions 100 percent. I also wanted to be accepted and was concerned about looking good. I had some control issues to sort out and feelings about abandonment. Some of this may sound familiar to anyone who is an adult child of an alcoholic. Several of us on the training team are adult children or spouses of alcoholics or are recovering from our own addictions. Discussing these issues in the training team has helped all of us. It is not always easy, yet I know if we do not discuss in a clear and assertive manner the meaningful things in our lives, we certainly cannot ask the participants to do it. At the end of three days, the team had built a community, worked on some of its issues, and made decisions about the content; that is, what to adapt or add or leave out.

At every event, the participants arrive eager and tentative, quietly watching or actively mingling, or any range of behaviors in between. The task of the team is to enlarge its community and find ways to include the many different women who have just arrived. As I had been met with all my vulnerability, we work at meeting the participants where they start from.

The first night sets a tone for the whole event. Here we ask, What do you want to get out of this experience and what do you think we can accomplish? Whatever hopes and fears we hear, we try to meet participants' needs. If we cannot revise our content for this particular training event, then perhaps their concerns will shape the next event. The training evolves each time we do it.

Another important part of the first night is the naming exercise. The first time I did a name tag that really focused all of my ambivalence over my name. I had legally changed it yet still wasn't happy with it. I grew up with so many different names: one for church and one for public school and a nickname. I had no middle name, just an initial. I used to dislike my first name—the "church version," I called it as I was growing up. I was called both by my legal name, Sandra, and by my baptismal name, Alessandra, "the Latin version of the Greek Alexander," I was told. After seeing the name *Alessandra* printed in a Spanish newspaper article, I changed my legal name to Alessandra, a combination of both versions.

At the training we make name tags that depict our names visually. I was frustrated to realize my name still was not right for me. I love the exercise because I see so many women learn something about themselves. I love the stories the women tell as they recount the history of their names. One woman said she used the name "Sue" because it is a version of her maiden name and helps her stay in touch with herself.

The naming exercise teaches me that is is OK to talk about myself and my beliefs, about my experiences of life. I know the experience must have an ongoing impact on participants' lives; it certainly has for me. During the writing of this piece, I have become convinced that I am going to change my name one more time and reach a resolution. I will rename myself ALEXSANDRA, and claim my own name out of my history and all of the things I have learned about it over the years. As a result of the training I have renamed, reclaimed, or reinvented many parts of my self. I have given up the self-contempt. Each time I refocus on who I am, I reclaim a part of me. The experience of community as begun with naming, allows each of us to open ourselves and move toward letting down the guard. In community I tell my story and see that I do not need to hang on to that old pain, the non-functioning way of relationship or the self-contemptual attitude. I think that many participants have done the same.

In fact, the name exercise introduces a key concept of the training: be fully yourself. One area during the training event in which this is realized is the module on spirituality. As explained in an earlier chapter, we use the definition of spirituality expressed by the lay theologian Verna Dozier. According to Verna, spirituality does not require us to be anything more than we are. Her definition emphasizes the power of being fully who we are in that moment, of claiming our choices and being fully aware of the costs as well as the promises.

As trainers, we share our stories with participants to help them reclaim their actual experiences. At one session, I recalled the words of a speaker I had heard years ago while on a retreat. Pointing to a tree outside the window, the speaker said, "Look at the tree. It is being the "treeiest" tree it knows how to be. It is being what God has asked it to be. The 'elmiest' elm, or the 'oakiest' oak, it knows how to be." Turning to the room full of participants, the speaker continued, "That is what God asks of you: to be the most you can be. The 'Annest' Ann you know how; the 'Sandiest' Sandy it is possible to become." At the training session, I talked about how this experience had made an impact on my life. If I cannot say who I am or claim autonomy, I do not have anything to give to others in the name of God. To be what I am called to be is to claim my spirituality.

I know that, for me, being fully in the moment—being aware—is a spiritual path. I have often longed for words with which to respond when someone says that it is not Christian to use "I" statements, that it is selfish. I have struggled when people dismiss assertive behavior as self-focused rather than a way to negotiate through the tangle of human relationships toward a clear mutual respect. I think that is loving behavior, and we are called to love others as ourselves. If I have not learned to love myself, to negotiate with respect for me, I do not think it is possible to love or respect others.

At a recent training session, one woman observed that being "fully herself" was a stewardship issue. I agree. "To be assertive, to manage myself, to be responsible for myself is simply being a good steward," she said. The training also helps participants discover that spirituality is a whole way of being, an attitude, a life. We notice what is nourishing us spiritually and continue that activity. We ask, What connects me to the creative spirit? When do I feel most alive and a part of that power?

I appreciate that the sessions do not hand out answers and prescriptions, although some people are looking for that. Sometimes I think evaluation comments like "the training was not spiritual enough" come from people who want an external guide. But the training is not designed to do this. Instead, we say that being fully me will be different from being fully you. The call to be you is different than what I discover when I respond to the call to discovering myself. Each woman's story is unique and uniquely hers.

As a trainer, it is fulfilling to watch others claim their spiritual path. I like watching women get excited about who they are and developing skills that will help them in their journey. I find it a sacramental act to participate in someone's learning, growing, and expanding.

One of the most significant recognitions I received recently was from a woman at a leadership training event who thanked me for my ministry. I was incredibly moved that she could see what I do in this training is a calling, when a close member of my family cannot. It was a gift, and I got tears in my eyes; it is so wonderful to be recognized.

For this book, we were asked to share stories or poems that would be appropriate expressions of our experience of the training. There are two for me, not in any priority order. The first expression is from a poem by Elizabeth Barrett Browning: "Earth is crammed with Heaven, and every bush is fired with God, but only those who see—take off their shoes."[1]

The second is a parable attributed to the Danish philosopher Sören Kierkegaard. It uses the numbers one through four to symbolize a journey toward wholeness, the developmental phases of an individual, with one being the least complex and four the most unified expression of personhood.

The parable speaks of four individuals. The first is a simple individual, perhaps a peasant, who gets up at sunrise, eats a bowl of rice or oats and goes about the daily tasks of living. For me, this is an unaware stage. It is not seeing who I am called to be. The second-dimensional person is rather like Don Quixote, tilting against windmills, sincere in the mission while not knowing what the mission is. The third stage, or third-dimensional person, is a Hamlet-like figure who is stuck in the dilemma of life. The fourth-dimensional person is the individual who has worked through complex issues, perhaps like Faust, who, after having sold his soul, is redeemed. On the surface, this person resembles the first-dimensional individual. She wakes in the dawn, eats her bowl of oatmeal, and goes about the tasks of daily living. But as she walks along the road, the trees blossom and bow down. For me, this means she is fully aware, and has sorted the important from the unimportant in her life. Her awareness of the moment, the ability to see what is fixed with God, has transformed her being, and the Spirit recognizes spirit.

Notes
1. Adapted from *Aurora Leigh,* by Elizabeth Barrett Browning.

EASING THE BUMPS OF REENTRY

Katherine Tyler Scott

We remembered the stories we had heard of people who had gone to training workshops or conferences and upon their return home had announced a major decision that affected many others. Some of these stories we knew from personal experience.

Many people and institutions are still reverberating from group experiences in the sixties and seventies. I can always tell if we are dealing with a casualty of such times when they say something like, "Is this going to be touchy-feely?" Touchy-feely is a code phrase for waste of time or dangerous. Either way the question is a cover for a negative experience the person is not wanting to repeat. The content and process used in our leadership training invites the risk of self-discovery, learning, and growth in a supportive, caring community that respects and values individual choice. We have all worked to achieve this kind of environment, and what we create is not what most of us have experienced or will return to after the training.

"After the training" became a key phrase as we remembered and recounted stories of experiences people have had. People had left intense group experiences—often positive transformational ones—and had returned to their familiar environments *unprepared* or ill-prepared for reentry. We knew we had a responsibility to enable participants to return to their homes, churches, and communities with a conscious knowledge of what they would experience, using our stories of reentry and suggestions for how to manage *after* the training. All that participants experienced would not be useful if it could only be experienced or accomplished in the leadership training sessions.

During our session on reentry, we acknowledge the changes, insights, growth, bonding, and cutting edges for future development, and we celebrate and affirm them. We acknowledge that we are ending this experience and provide opportunities for participants to say good-bye. An inability to acknowledge endings interferes with the capacity to begin anew. We all say good-bye differently. Our diversity in this respect is honored, but we call each other on behavior that denies the separation. One participant said in a most cheerful voice, "Let's not be sad; we'll be seeing each other at meetings!" Another said, "I don't know why we have to say good-bye. After all, we all live in this diocese. It's not as if we're not going to see each other again." In yet another community, a participant was emphatic: "I'm not going to say good-bye. I know our paths will cross again!" None of these comments disturbed me; I had used them myself at certain times in my life. I empathized with their feelings. It is difficult to learn that letting go enhances our ability to apply our learnings effectively. Letting go is an act of empowerment—of self and of others. The community we experienced over five days is disbanded. But what remains are the beliefs, values, attitudes, and gifts that helped create it and helped it to be inclusive. Many participants come to this recognition as they seek to integrate this experience into their "back home" lives.

Participants are asked to step into the shoes of those who have not been with them, i.e., spouses, children, friends, colleagues, employers. Life has gone on while we have taken this reflective respite, and a failure to be pastoral as we step back into this ongoing stream of life can be disastrous. We discuss ways to reconnect to significant people in our lives in ways that are respectful of us and of them. If your spouse has had to deal with a flooded basement, a sick kitten, and a crying child, you will not want to spend your first twenty minutes together sharing how wonderful it was to reclaim your full name or announce that you are no longer going to clean the bathroom. This is not the time to say, "I'm a ENTJ personality type. You're the total opposite of me—that's been our problem!" Judgmental pronouncements, labeling, or prescribing are not appropriate ways to communicate ever, and this is a time to say *never*.

Decisions that have an impact on others should be made in ways that include and consider them. Leadership training provides *preparation* for decision making; it is not the place to make life-altering choices that affect others with whom you live or work.

Participants are given time to plan how they want to go home, knowing that they will need to prepare to be flexible. In many instances, their home and work situations will not nurture their new behaviors, attitudes, or sense of self. In these cases, they are encouraged to seek support and affirmation elsewhere while they work on changing the situation. Leaders need support and affirmation, too.

I have facilitated the session on reentry a number of times, and it is always both sobering and humorous as we share our tales and envision the next steps of our journeys. I remember sharing an experience I had between two leadership training events. In this instance, I was appointed to a subcommittee of three to evaluate a diocesan program. The other two committee members were clergy. We scheduled several meetings, and when one of them could not attend, the meeting was changed. The next communication I received informed me that the two members had seen each other and decided what we were to do. As I reread my assignment, I saw that it bore little resemblance to what strengths I offered this responsibility. While I could have done the task, I did not feel good about the process. (My first reaction was to wish that my colleagues had attended leadership training. This helped me to avoid action for about fifteen minutes.) I knew that silence and compliance would not be congruent with my beliefs—they would be parties to disempowerment. I also knew that what I needed to do would be risky. I called both priests, explained in an assertive manner my feelings about the communique, and suggested that we meet *as a group* to decide together our work and tasks. We all had reasons for our difficulties in arranging a meeting: too busy, a wedding, two funerals, a crisis on the vestry, moving, two meetings, and on and on. Are we too busy to minister to each other, I wondered?

When we met, I shared my feelings about and wishes for how we could work together and get our job done. The two clergy recounted why they had decided without including me in their decision. After we talked, I understood. They then agreed I should be chairperson. I resisted; they insisted. I became *coordinator* in my own mind, but I was *chair* in theirs. I realized they were operating from a pyramid model of leadership, and I was based in the circular model. Someone had to be in charge: one of them or me. Selecting a top person to chair or be "in charge" does not really address the issue of *how* groups will work together, and the *how* was my chief concern. I realized that our basic beliefs about how people work together were not always the same and that my job was to work on listening and understanding our differences. A belief in the pyramid leaves little flexibility in choice-making. In such a model, clergy are at the top, and they are either in charge or they are not. Our inability to reach consensus on how we would work together and to affirm the importance of such a decision made the completion of this project very difficult. The project was done and, I think, proved useful in salvaging a diocesan program. And I learned a lesson for the hundredth time: it is hard to overcome the pyramid! Why did I persist? Because I truly believe that valuing and including the gifts of others leads to a stronger community and better products. In the face of conflicting values and environments, I had acted in concert with my beliefs. We must all face this challenge. Participants in the leadership training program are or will become acutely aware of discrepancies between beliefs and behavior upon their return home.

We each have a responsibility to behave with integrity and to model the beliefs we hold. I happen to believe that behavior that puts some "up" and others "down," that excludes and denies the gifts of others, does not belong anywhere, especially in the church. Leadership comes from both the clergy and laity and can be shared. I also believe that changing attitudes and beliefs takes time, but I will not give up my self or the power over my own behavior during this process. And I have shared with participants that at times the risk is high. They will frequently know when it is too high. The important thing is to make a choice about what *you* will do to make a difference. Being respectful, assertive, caring, and responsible will not guarantee you positive results. But you will be more fully *you*—more centered, confident, and effective as a leader. You then can manage the many reentries in life!

Questions for Reflection:
1. When you have had a new experience that changes the way you perceive, believe, or think, how do you let the significant people in your life know this?
2. How do you share your learnings and insights with others?
3. What are some ways you can use your learning to empower others?
4. Recall a situation when you asserted yourself. What happened? How did you maintain your self-esteem while respecting the other individual?
5. How can you experience reentry in ways that encourage growth in you and in those important to you?

SOME WORDS FROM PARTICIPANTS

The training shed light on the work that I need to do and clarified my goals. Holding up a mirror for my viewing was the experience I came to receive. I know myself better. My goal is to center on this new view.

◆

The Myers-Briggs test helped me to realize the differences in peoples' reactions, and my own assessment gave me insight into myself. I should be able to work with more understanding.

◆

Being the person I am—quiet, a serious thinker, and thoughtful—I do not speak out quickly enough. Often the group will assume that I am going along with all the decisions being made. But I know now that I must let them know in a very assertive way that I will not let them make a decision for me.

◆

The training made me more aware of our individual differences, yet our collective strength. A dynamic organization utilizes the talents of all. The discussions on empowerment gave me a more positive outlook on what can be accomplished when you are positive.

◆

The spirituality session didn't convey as much to me as I had hoped. But a truth that I had known but had never verbalized was spelled out—I am closest to God when I am the true me.

◆

After being out of the social work field for seven years, I will be reentering it this week and will lead some groups. I feel much better for the knowledge gained but especially for the opportunity to interact in groups again. I feel much better prepared.

◆

Before going to the training, I had hoped that I would be accepted as a woman who is good enough as she is and not incomplete because she is not a man. This hope was realized, and I felt a real affection for and appreciation of other women. Thank you.

I feared that I would be embarrassed, especially by positive feedback (which I am not used to). But we weren't generally put in embarrassing positions or asked to do anything embarrassing.

✦

I was afraid that I would be emotional and cry in front of the group. Well, I did cry, and it didn't bother anyone particularly, and I didn't die. I may try that again sometime. I was afraid that I would get tired of so much togetherness. I did, but that's OK because it's me. I'm afraid to go home, because I'll forget how this works and blow it out of the water many more times and still not be assertive. But that's OK because, if I succeed just once, it's one more time than I would have before. I'll work at it because I've got something to work at.

✦

The training brought me back in touch with myself, which is something I've always suppressed. I know now that it's not an accident that I don't like to lead. I wish now that I knew everyone's types [through the Myers-Briggs testing] so I would understand how to relate to them. I guess I can be a more effective leader now.

✦

Knowing that some needs come from a personality type and are not a judgment on me as a person frees me to lead. Knowing that I am OK just as I am frees me to lead using my skills, not the skills or feelings of a power person.

✦

The training helped me to deal with anger and to react and give feedback in a positive way rather than venting or holding it in.

✦

Most helpful for me was the exercise "The Blues and the Greens." That was a triple whammy. Not only did I find out that I wasn't who I thought I was, but what I considered perfectly acceptable behavior was actually passive-aggressive and destructive to the group. To top it off, I discovered that I had done just that last week at my church, which made someone thoroughly irritated with me.

✦

The exercises dealing with anger were most helpful, also the -isms role play. As a woman priest whose ordination is not recognized by four of my local colleagues, I learned how much energy it takes for them to continue to exclude me.

One of the finest long-term achievements of the leadership training is the network of women leaders across the state. My greatest satisfaction has been from the new friendships made and in the deepening of friendships.

✦

The training was a turning point in my life. It seems to be a year of major turning points, major life adjustments. I can really say that, from here out, nothing will ever be quite the same again. I'm glad you were all here—both the trainers and all the women that I didn't know but with whom I am a sister now. I pray for the day when we can drop the "women's" in "women's ministry" and the "woman" in "woman priest" and the "lady" in "lady bus driver." I praise God for allowing me, in my stonewalled militancy about feminism, to realize that the answer to that question—When am I most fully me?—was rather "feminine" and feeling. I was most complete when I held a friend in my arms and he cried; I could listen and help and soothe and protect and support. Writing was supposed to be my fulfillment, but I find it no worthy substitute for empty arms. I hope I have the stamina to deal with this insight and the grace to learn to be held as well as to hold.

BIOGRAPHIES

Dorothy J. Brittain has more than twenty years' experience as a consultant, trainer, and adult education specialist. She has designed and implemented training programs for government, churches, and nonprofit organizations. The author of several professional publications, she served for seven years as executive director of the Association for Creative Change in Religious and Other Social Systems. Dorothy lives in Brewerton, New York.

Edna M. Brown is a senior associate of EDB Consulting Group, Inc., a management development and training company. Edna is also an experienced professional consultant, manager, and author. In her professional career, she has written successful proposals and managed grant-funded projects for several major foundations and the federal government. Also, she has developed and presented seminars and workshops on obtaining grants, writing proposals, project development, leadership development, and supervisory skills. Since the inception of the Women of Vision program, she has been active as a developer and trainer.

Sally Bucklee is an experienced manager and internal consultant with the Prince George's County Health Department in Maryland. She also serves as consultant, trainer, and seminar leader to nonprofit, voluntary, health care, and religious systems. One of the early advocates for both the ordination of women and the ministry of the laity, Sally was organizer and cochair of the international Women's Witnessing Community, sponsored by the Episcopal Women's Caucus, at the 1988 Lambeth Conference of Anglican bishops in England. An ENTP (Myers-Briggs Type Indicator), she and her husband, Brian, live in Laurel, Maryland (where their rector is a woman!), in a home abandoned by one daughter and one son under mutually loving terms.

Linda L. Grenz was ordained in 1977 and served as the rector of St. Paul's, Camden, Delaware, until 1984. Linda served as a consultant with the Women in Mission and Ministry office after having established her own consulting business working with banks and small businesses. She is currently the associate director of the Overseas Development Office of the Episcopal Church, where she works with Anglican partners in Africa, Asia, and Latin America to develop the human and financial resources of the church to work in solidarity with the poor and oppressed.

Katherine Tyler Scott is a consultant/trainer for human service organizations, businesses, and churches, specializing in organizational and leadership development. She developed the Lilly Endowment Leadership Education Program and currently directs the Trustee Leadership Development Program, a statewide resource and training program for nonprofit boards in Indiana. She helped develop the WIMM leadership training and the Women of Vision training for the Episcopal Church Women. Katherine, an active member of Trinity Episcopal Church in Indianapolis, serves on several commissions and committees at both the diocesan and national levels. Her vocation is to empower both individuals and institutions to become more caring and serving. Katherine is married to Fred, a wonderful tax attorney and is the proud mother of a eighteen-year-old. Sharing with family and friends, reading, and writing poetry are her favorite pastimes.

Ann Smith is the executive for Women in Mission and Ministry, a program unit at the national Episcopal Church.

Before this job, she was the founder and director of Women's Work, a community-based women's organization that trained and placed poor women in nontraditional jobs with the building trade unions. She also served on the commission on the status of women for the State of Connecticut. She and her husband, Whitney, have two grown daughters. Ann, Whitney, two cats, and a dog live in Westport, Connecticut.

Eleanor Smith is an illustrator, writer, and professional volunteer. She is the founding art editor of the Journal of Women's Ministries, which is published by the Council for Women's Ministries of the Episcopal Church, and the creator of the comic strip "Jane" in that publication. She currently serves as program cabinet coordinator for the Diocese of Oklahoma and serves on the national boards of the Episcopal Historical Society, Episcopal Women's History Project, the Church Periodical Club, and the National Altar Guild.

Alexsandra K. Stewart is an independent consultant who works with a variety of clients in government, education, and the private sector—both internationally and in the United States. She specializes in gender and racial issues, the appreciation and management of diversity, and organizational development. A resident of Washington, D.C., Alexsandra is a member of a multicultural, multi-ethnic, and diverse family system.

Claire Woodley is an Episcopal priest in the Diocese of New York. She has worked with the Women in Mission and Ministry unit as both staff and consultant. Most recently she has worked on the Episcopal participation in the Ecumenical Decade for Churches in Solidarity with Women. She is currently working on family issues, intergenerational relationships and community building. Claire is married to Michael Aitchison; they have a son, Noah, who is the light of her life.

◆

Marcy Darin currently edits the *Journal of Women's Ministries*, which is published by the Council for Women's Ministries of the Episcopal Church. She is a former editor in the Office of Communication at the Episcopal Church Center in New York City and a freelance writer whose work has appeared in *The New York Times* and *Ms.* magazine. Marcy lives in Methuen, Massachusetts, with her husband, Glenn Chalmers, an Episcopal priest; daughter Abigail; and son Aaron.